Dining at the Master's Table
Learning to Hear the Voice of the Lord

Paul D. Norcross

*My sheep hear my voice, and I know them,
and they follow me:*
John 10:27

D0057393

Second Printing
ISBN   **0-9671353-0-3**
Library of Congress Catalog Card No. : **99-93178**

Published By:
Kingdom Presence Publishing
PO Box 725
Charlemont, MA 01339
USA
Tel: (413) 339-8630
E-mail: Kingdom8@Juno.com *
Web Site: http://www.kingdomfaith.org

Printed in the USA by
MORRIS PUBLISHING
3212 East Highway 30 • Kearney, NE 68847 • 1-800-650-7888

Dedication

I have dedicated this book to my many teachers in the Lord. First and foremost is my Lord and Savior, Jesus Christ, who is still *The* Teacher. Next to Him, I owe profound thanks to my parents, Marian and Edmund, my wife Rita, and to so many other men and women of God who have lovingly and patiently helped me grow to hear His voice.

Finally, and with great joy, I dedicate this book to all those who long to know the pleasure and treasure of dining at the Master's table, in the presence of the King. May it be a contribution toward helping God's people overcome and be invited to sit with the Lord in His throne (Revelation 3:21).

Acknowledgments

This book has certainly been a labor of love. I can't imagine undertaking such a project without the Lord's loving guidance, wisdom, and leading. He has worked in so many wonderful fellow ministers, without whose wise counsel and diligent efforts in editing, evaluating, and giving, this book could not have been written. May our Lord Jesus Christ, our King, reward them all abundantly!

Contents

Foreward

Christianity is not a set of rules and doctrines, but a living relationship of truth and love with our Father, His Son our Lord, and the Holy Spirit. One of the great desires of our Lord is to have intimate communication with every man, woman, and child in His church.

In *Dining at the Master's Table: Learning to Hear the Voice of the Lord,* Paul shows Scriptural truths concerning our relationship with the Lord and hearing His voice. He additionally draws from his own experience to illustrate the practical nature of these truths in order to help Christians learn to hear the voice of the Lord, to know His plans for their lives, and help them to see their place in the body of Christ.

As in all things of the Spirit, a person's flesh will want to fight the teaching in these pages. Flesh will say, "It's too easy to be true", or "I'm not good enough yet." But the Lord clearly desires intimate fellowship with His people, and such fellowship is available to all of them.

Dining at the Master's Table is simple, refreshing, and encouraging to those who desire to walk with the Lord, enjoying His presence in their lives. As revealed in the pages of this book, there are no shortcuts, but neither is there any comparison to the pleasure of His company around His table.

Steve Strzepek

Introduction

Mutsuko Yoneda couldn't ignore the voice of the Lord any longer. For three months He had been urging her to flee the city and go to the hills. Within her spirit, the Lord's insistence was so loud that she knew she must not delay. Mutsuko packed up her children, and explained to her sister-in-law employer what the Lord had said. That night she found lodging far away in the mountains. The next morning, the city of Hiroshima was no more[i].

Trusting the Lord's Voice
Mutsuko had learned to trust the voice of the Lord. She had built her relationship with Him such that she recognized His voice, and elected to obey it. There were other Christians in Hiroshima. The Lord is no respecter of persons (Romans 2:11; Ephesians 6:9). He certainly tried to get through to each one of His children. Some of them did not hear.

Proverbs 3:5
Trust in the LORD with all thine heart; and lean not unto thine own understanding. In all thy ways acknowledge him, and he shall direct thy paths.

The word "trust" includes a sense of "to confide in." When we confide in the Lord, we share our heart with Him. For the Lord to direct our paths, we must be willing to listen. Many Christians bring their troubles to the Lord, and their overwhelming preoccupation with them drowns out the Lord's direction, advice, teaching, and counsel.

Preoccupation with self instead of preoccupation with praise and worship produces anemic results. A self-burdened heart prays the problem. But a praise-burdened heart continually praises God for His solutions and gets results.

A heart that is dwelling on problems holds them higher than God, higher than His ability to solve them. This is the result of pride, not humility. On the other hand, a heart of praise is a heart of humility. God resists pride. His grace goes to the humble (I Peter 5:5 and 6). The people who come to Him according to His standard (praise and thanksgiving), not their own standard (focus on self, unthankfulness), are the ones who are given more grace. Please don't misunderstand – God hears the cries of His people! It's just that His voice and loving fellowship are able to penetrate hearts prepared with praise.

So how can a Christian begin to build his or her relationship with the Lord such that they learn how He works within their spirit? Paul did it by spending his first three years after conversion "alone" with the Lord in Arabia. Jesus Christ learned how our Father worked within Him during his 40 days in the wilderness. The Lord teaches the way as we learn to draw close to Him.

Drawing Closer to Him
The best way I know to begin to draw close to Him is to spend time daily praising and worshipping the Father. When you faithfully come to Him, you will be astonished at the deepening of your fellowship with Jesus, and the amount of direction He'll provide.

Psalms 100:4
Enter into his gates with thanksgiving, and into his courts with praise: be thankful unto him, and bless his name.

Entering His gates and His courts refers to the innermost sanctum of the temple, where God lived in the Old Testament.

Introduction

One time a year, the high priest entered the holy of holies to commune with God. If the priest entered with sin and uncleanness, he would not survive the entrance. He would be killed. Today, as a result of our confession of Jesus as Lord[1] we are his habitation[2] and we can have an audience with Him. But we will not often enter a close fellowship with Him in our prayer closet if it is not preceded by thanksgiving, praise, and repentance for our sins.

Our offering today is the praise of our lips.[3] Praise out of a thankful heart opens the access to the Lord's fellowship. He will speak volumes in the quiet, worshipful stillness of our spirit. Matthew 7:18-25 contains sobering truths for Christians

---

[1] *Romans 10:9-10*
That if thou shalt confess with thy mouth the Lord Jesus, and shalt believe in thine heart that God hath raised him from the dead, thou shalt be saved.
For with the heart man believeth unto righteousness; and with the mouth confession is made unto salvation.

[2] *1 Corinthians 6:19*
What? know ye not that your body is the temple of the Holy Ghost which is in you, which ye have of God, and ye are not your own?
Ephesians 2:21-22
In whom all the building fitly framed together groweth unto an holy temple in the Lord:
In whom ye also are builded together for an habitation of God through the Spirit.

[3] *Hebrews 13:15*
By him therefore let us offer the sacrifice of praise to God continually, that is, the fruit of our lips giving thanks to his name.
1 Peter 2:9
But ye are a chosen generation, a royal priesthood, an holy nation, a peculiar people; that ye should shew forth the praises of him who hath called you out of darkness into his marvellous light:

who have not learned to hear the voice of Jesus our Lord, and of our heavenly Father.

Matthew 7:21-25
Not every one that saith unto me, Lord, Lord, shall enter into the kingdom of heaven; but he that doeth the will of my Father which is in heaven.
Many will say to me in that day, Lord, Lord, have we not prophesied in thy name? and in thy name have cast out devils? and in thy name done many wonderful works?
And then will I profess unto them, I never knew you: depart from me, ye that work iniquity.
Therefore whosoever heareth these sayings of mine, and doeth them, I will liken him unto a wise man, which built his house upon a rock:
And the rain descended, and the floods came, and the winds blew, and beat upon that house; and it fell not: for it was founded upon a rock.

Spending Time with the Lord
How are we going to hear His sayings and do them if we are not spending time close to His lips? How are we going to know him (literally to know by experience) so that He will not be able to say "I never knew you" - i.e. I never had an active, ongoing relationship with you - if we are not regularly spending time dining at the Master's table?

The same thought is expressed in Peter's inspired response to the men of Israel who marveled at the lame man's healing at the Beautiful gate in Acts 3.

Acts 3:19-24
*Repent ye therefore, and be converted, that your sins may be blotted out, **when the times of refreshing shall come from the presence of the Lord;***

Introduction

And he shall send Jesus Christ, which before was preached unto you:
Whom the heaven must receive **until the times of restitution of all things,** which God hath spoken by the mouth of all his holy prophets since the world [aion, meaning "age"] began.
For Moses truly said unto the fathers, A prophet shall the Lord your God raise up unto you of your brethren, like unto me; **him shall ye hear in all things whatsoever he shall say unto you.**
And it shall come to pass, that every soul, which will not hear that prophet, shall be destroyed from among the people.
Yea, and all the prophets from Samuel and those that follow after, as many as have spoken, have likewise foretold of these days.

I used to read these verses of Peter's speech and presume they were all fulfilled by Jesus Christ's life on earth, prior to Pentecost only. But notice verse 21, referring to the restitution (*apokatastasis* meaning "to restore to a former state"[ii]) of all things. Since this restoration has not yet occurred, these verses in Acts 3 are clearly still being fulfilled even today. My point is this – Jesus is still talking to believers today, and we are to hear His voice today. We are to hear all things whatsoever He shall say to us *today*, not only His words recorded in the Scripture.

Revelation 3:20
Behold, I stand at the door, and knock: **if any man hear my voice,** and open the door, **I will come in to him, and will sup** [fellowship] **with him, and he with me.**

Perhaps you have known these principles and have personally seen the benefits of faithfully applying them in the past, but somehow the fire has died down. The routines and hectic schedules you face all work against spending time alone with

7

the Lord. Of course they do! Satan tries to see to it. So what can you do about it?

You Can Build A Fire With The Lord's Help
In cold weather the first thing I often do when I wake up is go down to the basement and re-build the wood stove fire. The embers have burned down overnight, and new wood needs to be added. But even before the new wood goes on, sometimes I need to begin by shoveling out the old ashes, and rebuild with dry kindling. I might need to blow on it to flare up the embers and ignite the tinder. In other words, I have to work with it to make flames appear. The few glowing coals that remain don't produce much heat.

We have to work with the Lord each day to keep our fire going. Some of us go a whole day with a cold stove before finally figuring out the reason why we feel distant from the Lord.

Some will add sweaters of phone calls to spiritual confidants. Others will stomp their feet and remark that their spiritual temperature is falling. They'll briskly try to rub the spiritual cold from their arms by reading countless testimonials, or try to warm themselves at someone else's fire by attending endless seminars. They'll see frosty breath and wonder where the Lord's fire went – all because they forgot to build their own hearth fire each morning with Him.

To make flames appear, we need to use good wood, seasoned with a humble confession of sin (I John 1:9), and placed over the kindling of praise and worship. We need to blow on the flames - perhaps gently, or maybe fervently - according to the leading of the Lord, and we need to refresh ourselves in the warmth of His flame as the fire takes off. Curiously with my wood stove, I have to refresh it every morning if I expect to be warm for the day. Jesus did it. Shouldn't we?

Introduction

Mark 1:35
And in the morning, rising up a great while before day, he went out, and departed into a solitary place, and there prayed.

God is not going to knock you over the head to tell you things He reserves for the quiet warmth of your hearthfire. He didn't yell at Moses or Abraham or Samuel. Instead he attracted Moses' attention with the burning bush. Moses took his shoes off and paid heed. Abraham could have remained in Haran in the comfort of the family business, and Samuel could have rolled over and gone back to sleep each time he heard the voice of the Lord. Ananias could have continued minding his own business and ignored the Lord's message to go minister to the future apostle Paul. Mutsuko Yoneda didn't just happen to wake up one morning to hear the Lord talking to her.

All these people had built an ongoing relationship with the Lord, making Him their best friend. In so doing, they had learned to trust His voice. Such trust is not built by occasional visits. Trust comes from a relationship built over frequent heart-to-heart sharings. Why not frequent Jesus' fireside?

Knowing Him
John 10:27
My sheep hear my voice, and I know them, and they follow me:

The word for "know" here in John 10:27 is the same word as in Matthew 7:23. It means to know by experience, i.e. to have a relationship. Those who don't know the sound of the Chief Shepard's voice do not have a relationship with Him that is sufficiently developed. A common result is a low intensity fire – embers that are lukewarm. Sheep must hear the voice of the Shepherd.

Introduction

We are all tempted with lifestyles that are too busy; ones that crowd the Master's time alone with us. We long for the warmth of His counsel by the hearth fire of His heart. We want to eat a full meal at His table, but instead if we sit down at all, it is only to snack.

God won't build this fire for us – that's our job each morning. But what joy it is to spend time alone with Him in His presence as He helps us take our little embers, and helps us fan them into a daily spiritual bonfire. The words He shares at His fireplace will include the words of revelation we need to help build His church (Matthew 16:13-19) and prevent the gates of hell from prevailing against it. This is how we get our revelation manna for each day. This is how we are to grow up into Him – at His fireside, dining at His table.

May God continue to reveal His Son in you each day as you approach Him in praise and worship, learning the certainty of His voice in your spirit.

Responsibility to The Lord

No individual can possibly carry the burden and the responsibility to teach a subject such as this without specific direction from the Lord. The consequences of misunderstanding the message both as a reader and as an author are critical if even one person becomes hurt in their walk before the Lord. This is my greatest concern as I present this material before God's people. All of us long to draw closer to our Lord and Savior, to hear the comfort of His encouragement, His instruction, and His chastening as a patient big brother, intercessor, lord and judge.

And yet for some of His children, the concept and reality of an intimate relationship with the Master may be elusive. In the excitement of a fellow believer's revelation from the Lord, there is room in the hearer's mind to feel hurt – "why doesn't the Lord talk to me that way?" The answer is not in divine favoritism, because God doesn't have favorites. The answer is in the hearthfire. The Holy Spirit will help you build it as you join yourself to Him.

But one caution presents itself in the process of learning how to hear the voice of the Lord: *do not take another person's experience as the standard.* What is presented as doctrinal in these chapters is from the best of my ability and my understanding of Scripture as the Lord has led me. Though I am confident of the doctrine and have a deep, continual longing to grow further in Him, my experiences and those of others presented in this book need to be viewed only as illustration, not as doctrine. Doctrine and experience can never become mixed, because to presume the Lord will work with you in precisely the same manner as He does with someone else is a quick route to spiritual frustration. Let the Holy Spirit guide you. That is why He has been sent.

A second note is needed regarding how God chooses to communicate to His people. Revelation comes in many ways. To some, the Lord communicates most effectively through visions and dreams. Some may find they receive revelation most often while they are alone driving in their car, or even in the shower. Some see clear pictures while others have learned that revelation comes to them as an inner knowing, a clear certainty in their spirit. For still others, revelation is received as a voice inside, and to others, rarer perhaps, it is an audible voice outside themselves.

This book is not about cataloging the myriad ways in which God can and does communicate with His people today. Rather, it is a book about faithfully keeping appointments with the Master, and in so doing, learning to enjoy dining in intimate fellowship around His table. The blessings garnered from such fellowship include much closer communication with the Lord through His voice to you. Therefore, this book is not about the Lord's ability and capacity to communicate at seemingly random times and in various ways, occasionally penetrating into the midst of your busy lifestyle. Instead, it is a book about developing a lifestyle *in* Him, one that is focused on faithfully and regularly entering His presence and participating in the abundance of revelation manna which flows therefrom. It is a book about pursuing a relationship, not an experience.

May God bless you abundantly as you read and consider His heart behind the pages of this book. My fervent desire is that it will help intensify the depth of your fellowship with the One who is always knocking at your door, Who so longingly desires to sit down with you at His table, and share the deep secrets of His life and vision for you daily.

SECTION I

Jesus is Knocking - Will You Open the Door?

Chapter 1

How I Learned to Hear The Lord's Voice

Rita and I were newly married in December 1975. After a few short weeks together she returned to nursing school for her spring semester, and I continued my navy training. By spring I was assigned as gunnery officer aboard a frigate. Rita joined me to re-begin married life together in Norfolk, Virginia in May 1976. So we thought.

On June 6 the ship was scheduled to deploy to the Mediterranean for six months. We prayed until we were blue in the face that the ship would somehow stay put. Nevertheless, on the appointed day we slipped the pier and steamed down the harbor channel for what seemed like an eternity to newlyweds.

After a few days of extremely long work hours with both my 20-man division as well as watches on the bridge at night, I felt I would die spiritually if I didn't start a Bible fellowship on board. I asked God for one person to share the Word with that day. That afternoon, a young seaman boatswain's mate and I spoke during my duty in the ship's combat information center. He was excited about what the Lord could teach him, and we set a date for two nights later to meet to share God's Word in our off time.

The time came and I hadn't seen "Mouse," as the crew called him, in the intervening days. Five minutes after the time set to meet, he hadn't showed and I was beginning to wonder. Cramped in the tiny space of the gunnery office, I began to read my Bible. Soon a knock came at the door, and in walked Mouse and a friend he had witnessed to after our initial conversation. Our first fellowship began! By the end of the following year, the Lord had built this beginning into three active fellowships with over 30 wonderful saints.

Not all was roses. The work was demanding, and often stretched into 20 hour days and more, seven days a week. Each person in the fellowship had jobs to do around the clock. Scheduling anything was impossible, and I quickly learned to ask the Lord at the close of each fellowship when the next one should be. He always inspired an answer, and it was always at a time when everyone could attend. Sometimes we would have just one fellowship a week. Other times it would be four or five. But when asked, the Lord always provided an answer. I learned the hard way that asking Him is always fruitful. Deciding on my own brought only marginal results at best.

Hearing His Voice
One night was particularly memorable. I finished a watch on the bridge at midnight but still couldn't sleep. I was too wired from four hours of nearly continuous speaking in tongues as I performed my duties. At such times it was often peaceful on the ocean with no other ships near by. It was easy to speak in perfect praise to God and pray for my fellow brothers in Christ in the decks below. When it came time to be relieved from the watch, I left to walk the upper decks and commune with the Lord before going to sleep.

I found a bollard and sat down. A bollard is a large pipe-like protrusion that sticks up through the deck. Capped off with a steel plate about 24 inches high, it is used to attach mooring lines when the ship is tied up at a pier. Bollards are positioned right next to the side rail lines on every ship, and they form a perfect seat to view the passing ocean just over the side. Sitting on a bollard at sea is like the Eastern custom of sitting under an oak tree – it's a peaceful place to reflect in the midst of an otherwise busy environment.

Although there were by now several other crew members and one other officer who had become born again, there was no one to whom I could go for spiritual counsel. But sitting on the bollard that night taught me something I'll never forget.

I began to pour my heart out to God. I missed Rita, and was weary from several weeks at sea. I was thankful, but getting worn down. At one point in my conversation to God, an inner voice told me to look up at the stars. They were beautiful, and the moon was as bright as I'd ever seen. In a quiet voice within that I knew was not from my own thoughts, the Lord said, "Paul, do you see the stars up there? Do you see the moon?" I paused, and then He said, "I put them up there for you."

I melted inside. God was reassuring me that He was always there, and that my life was important to Him. I knew from Psalms 19:1-6 that the stars and the planets were all in their positions for the specific purpose of announcing God's plan. But I hadn't thought of how particular they were for me, and for all of God's children.

But even more important, it was the first time I clearly knew the Lord's voice to me. To this day, even though I now spend time with the Lord every day, and treasure His voice to me just as much as I did that night, this incident is still among the most precious reminders of the love God has for me. In Matthew 10:30 and Luke 12:7 the Scriptures declare that the Father has numbered every hair on our heads. Can He be any less concerned about both the joys and burdens of your heart?

Psalms 139:1-10
O LORD, thou hast searched me, and known me.
Thou knowest my downsitting and mine uprising, thou understandest my thought afar off.
Thou compassest my path and my lying down, and art acquainted with all my ways.
For there is not a word in my tongue, but, lo, O LORD, thou knowest it altogether.
Thou hast beset me behind and before, and laid thine hand upon me.
Such knowledge is too wonderful for me; it is high, I cannot attain unto it.
Whither shall I go from thy spirit? or whither shall I flee from thy presence?
If I ascend up into heaven, thou art there: if I make my bed in hell, behold, thou art there.
If I take the wings of the morning, and dwell in the uttermost parts of the sea;
Even there shall thy hand lead me, and thy right hand shall hold me.

The Impact of Prayer

I learned that prayer for even inanimate things works! For example, my predecessor over the gunnery division had a nickname – Ltjg Boomclick. Frequently when the 5 inch gun mount was fired, a micro switch would fail and the round never left the barrel. When everyone expected the mount to fire with a huge "boom", often the only sound would be "click". Ever since the ship was new it had only shot competitive exercise scores in the 60's and 70's on a one hundred point scale. When I took over the job, the same fire control and gunnery maintenance personnel were still there. But the thing I did differently was prayer.

From my battle station high above the ship in the gun radar director station, I could look down on the forward gun mount and speak in tongues for the system to work properly and the gun to shoot accurately. Our scores rose. Each time we competed thereafter in annual ship exercises, our scores averaged 95 – nearly perfect. Prayer and the blessing of God was the only difference.

I didn't fully recognize the impact prayer had until years later when, as a lieutenant commander in the reserves, I was stationed for two weeks of annual training duty in the office of the headquarters of the Atlantic Fleet – the office that happened to keep the competitive exercise results of all the ships on the East coast. While there, I looked up the scores of my old ship. The records confirmed the early low scores, and the high scores during my tenure. To my astonishment they also showed a return to the same low scores once I had left the ship for new duties. By this time it was several years later, and the gun mount never again performed as well as it did under prayer. I was continuing to learn to depend on the Lord for help.

Obeying Him

Eventually the ship received a new commanding officer. By this time, I had moved on to a new job onboard, but the fellowship continued to grow. By now enough miracles had happened among crew members – healings, former drug users turning to the Lord and renouncing their former habits, lazy workers turning into model petty officers, etc. – that it was well known across the ship. The former commanding officer was a wonderful man who strongly supported the fellowship once he saw the results. He even attended a service and left with tears in his eyes.

When the new replacement commanding officer reported aboard, things changed almost immediately. The new captain soon ordered me to cease running Christian fellowships aboard his ship. So I took them "underground".

One night I was summoned to his stateroom at 4am to discuss a ridiculously inconsequential problem. Then he launched into the real reason for the summons. I was told that running Christian fellowships was illegal unless done by his permission and only on Sundays. How dare I run fellowships in opposition to his direct orders! After threatening me with a court martial for disobedience of a direct order, he challenged me with a parting taunt, "Why don't you just ask your God if you can't run fellowships on Sunday just like everyone else in the world does?" I said I would certainly ask and left his room. Dismissed.

God is Not Mocked
Out to the bollard again. I couldn't sleep, and felt like my stomach had been ripped out. Disheartened and discouraged, I cried out in the darkness to the Lord. I watched the faint glow of white off the bow wave as it washed aft along the side. After listening patiently to me, the Lord began speaking. His quiet inner voice assured me, "I will strengthen and upgird you, and I will not be mocked."

Two nights later on the bridge I noticed the captain in his chair. I knew I was supposed to communicate the words the Lord had spoken to me. It was dark in the pilothouse. I said, "Excuse me Captain." "What is it, Ltjg Norcross?" he replied. I told him I had done as he had requested and had asked the Lord why I couldn't run fellowships only on Sunday as he thought I should. Then I said, "Here's what the Lord told me: I will strengthen and upgird you, and I will not be mocked". The captain came out of his chair. In the meekest moment I had ever seen from this otherwise prideful man, he said in astonishment, "The Lord said that to you?" I continued to run fellowships aboard that ship without repercussions – at least not from him.

One time during a long refit period in a shipyard in England we had scheduled a Bible class that took several hours each day to complete. The class occurred at a time we were in a three week long refit period in Portsmouth, England. After one class session, one of my electricians came to me with a puzzled look on his face. "What's wrong?" I asked. He inquired whether anything had happened to the lights in the electrical room while we were running the class. I told him that they were fine. He mentioned he had pulled the fuses to the room while the class was in session in order to "play a joke" on us. Now, electricians know what they are doing with fuses. He was appalled that the lighting circuits never even flickered even though the circuit fuses were completely removed! I rejoiced. I decided to ignore the insubordinate action. The Lord was convicting him already.

Learning Not to Let God Down

One afternoon we had anchored in the Gulf of Solum off the coast of Libya. It was a relatively high spot in international waters which both Soviet and US ships used as an anchorage for non-portside repairs and upkeep. A mile off our starboard side anchored another destroyer from our squadron. This ship had the squadron commander aboard, an admiral, who was slated to visit our ship that day. But there was a problem. The helicopters of both ships were down for maintenance, and the sea was too choppy to launch a small boat. The admiral was stuck without a ride.

I had walked on deck onto the fantail, the aft part of the stern deck. I approached my executive officer and weapons officer who were at the rail gazing across to the other ship. The moment I walked up, the XO raised his arm and said, "Wouldn't it be great to be able to calm the sea?" I didn't know if he had said this to poke fun at me, or if he was serious, but just then the Lord told me to do it – to command the sea and wind to die down.

"But Lord," I said, "what if it doesn't happen? My superior officers will think I'm nuts and throw me off the ship." Quickly the Lord responded and said, "I will do it if you claim it in my name." I argued twice more and the moment passed. I felt I had let God down, and I felt crushed. I know to this day that if I had the faith to do the revelation that the Lord gave me, some awesome things would have happened. To this day, I still imagine myself telling the XO after calming the sea and wind in the name of Jesus Christ, "XO, tell the captain he has five hours with the admiral and not a minute more!"

But the moment had passed. The two other officers walked away, and I was left alone at the rail. In my sorrow I told God that if He ever gave me revelation like that again, I would never again crater in fear.

A Second Chance
About five hours later I was back on watch on the bridge. By this time we had weighed anchor and were steaming northeast toward Crete. A fog had rolled in that was so thick we couldn't even see the bow. Fog horns were sounded as required by international law, and we stationed a man with a radio handset up on the bow to keep watch. At sea, because it can take miles of ocean to stop a ship and because radars can fail, fog is a dangerous condition even out in open waters.

Nevertheless, it was quiet on the bridge. The status board keeper, helmsman, lee helmsman, and boatswains mate of the watch were each quietly performing their duties, and some were conversing in low tones. I was standing at the bridge window, peering through the fog when the Lord whispered, "Paul, it's available to lift the fog". I was delighted. Here I had just let God down a few hours earlier on the fantail. It felt wonderful that God was giving me something to do – I felt like God was giving me another chance.

In a quiet, non-interruptive voice, I whispered to the window, "God, thank you for getting rid of the fog in the name of Jesus Christ." I hadn't learned yet to simply claim things with the authority Jesus has already given to us, so at this time I was still asking God whenever acting on His revelation to me.

A few seconds elapsed. Nothing happened. Then God said, "That was good, Paul, and I'm going to do it. But I want you say it again a little louder." No problem. It was still just me and the bridge window. I could easily go up a few decibels without exposing myself. I tried it again. "God, in the name of Jesus Christ, thanks for getting rid of the fog."

This time I felt like the Lord was patting me on the shoulder as I realized nothing happened again. "That's good, Paul", He said again in my spirit, "but this time I want you to say it loud enough for the whole bridge to hear." I started to sink in my heart. "But Lord…," was as far as I managed to respond before He flashed across my mind the vow I had made earlier on the fantail –"If you ever give me revelation like that again, I promise I will never crater." I knew I had to shout it out, and the only way I'd know for sure the Lord was behind this was by doing it.

Out of the quiet busy-ness of the bridge, I shouted, "GOD, IN THE NAME OF JESUS CHRIST, THANKS FOR GETTING RID OF THE FOG!" The bridge went silent.

Suddenly I felt like I had a 1,000 watt light bulb heating up the back of my neck. All the conversations stopped. I kept looking out the window, my back to the rest of the bridge. Nothing happened.

At that point, what do you do? I decided I'd better pretend to go about business as usual. I peered into the dark hood over the radar repeater next to me, and watched the scope make a full trace around its face. Only two or three seconds had passed, but they seemed like an eternity. The status board keeper was the first to yell out, "Wow!"

I looked up to see the fog completely lifted from the ship. In fact it had receded a full five miles out to form a ring completely around the ship, and inside the circle was bright sunshine. We were all amazed. A few moments later the fog watch detail was secured. The fog stayed like a wall five miles out in all directions until the remainder of my watch – another 45 minutes. The moment I left the bridge to strike below after completing my watch, the fog rolled back over the ship and remained for several more hours.

Let The Lord Lift the Fog
I believe the Lord wants to lift the fog in the life of each and every one of His people. I believe He wants to teach each one how to be sure of His voice to them. He did it with Moses via the burning bush. He did it with Samuel as a young boy learning to minister before the Lord in the temple. I believe He will do it with you in order that you can learn how to hear His voice – how it sounds to your spirit. It will be different for you

than it has been for me, just like for Samuel it was very different than for Moses – and for Paul, for the apostle John, and for that "certain disciple," Ananias.

You are no less important to the Lord. I believe His desire to commune with you is not just the longing of your heart, but of His too. My prayer is that this book will in some way help you to learn the joy of hearing, trusting, and obeying the Master's voice. This is the treasure that the psalmist so desperately valued in Psalms 119 when he sang,

Thy testimonies also are my delight and my counsellors. (v24)

Remember the word unto thy servant, upon which thou hast caused me to hope. (v49)

This is my comfort in my affliction: for thy word hath quickened me. (v50)

The law of thy mouth is better unto me than thousands of gold and silver. (v72)

How sweet are thy words unto my taste! yea, sweeter than honey to my mouth! (v103)

Thy word is a lamp unto my feet, and a light unto my path. (v105)

Remember: The Lord is more anxious to talk to you than you are to talk to Him. He will lead you into a deeper relationship and His route will be different for you than it is for others because each of His children are unique. I have used my example simply to illustrate how the Lord chose to work with me. God has an individual training program specially for you, so don't be concerned if the experiences of others are not the same as yours. I pray that you will be able to write a much better book than this with sharings of how the Lord works with you!

Chapter 2

How The Lord Can Build His Church Through You

Before investigating how the Lord can work through you to build His church, let's take a look at how He taught this subject to the disciples. The following verses have often been viewed to mean that Christ builds His church, and of course this is quite true. But there is a deeper truth regarding His *method* for building which becomes clear in the context.

Matthew 16:13-18
When Jesus came into the coasts of Caesarea Philippi, he asked his disciples, saying, Whom do men say that I the Son of man am?
And they said, Some say that thou art John the Baptist: some, Elias; and others, Jeremias, or one of the prophets.
He saith unto them, But whom say ye that I am?
And Simon Peter answered and said, Thou art the Christ, the Son of the living God.
*And Jesus answered and said unto him, **Blessed art thou, Simon Barjona: for flesh and blood hath not revealed it unto thee, but my Father which is in heaven.***

Good job Peter! The Lord commended Peter for his answer because he received it by revelation from the Father. God wants to give revelation to his children – after all, three of the nine manifestations of the gift of holy spirit listed in I Corinthians 12 concern receiving revelation (word of knowledge, word of wisdom, and discerning of spirits). Revelation sounds like a big deal, but God never intended for it to be so. Like any Father, He wants to be able to talk with His children openly and often. Peter was learning how this worked for perhaps the first time.

Jesus Teaches Church-Building Strategy

Then Jesus said something in the context of hearing revelation from the Father. He outlined an astonishing plan for the future construction of the worldwide church.

Matthew 16:18-19
*And I say also unto thee, That thou art Peter, **and upon this rock I will build my church**; and the gates of hell shall not prevail against it.*
And I will give unto thee the keys of the kingdom of heaven: and whatsoever thou shalt bind on earth shall be bound in heaven: and whatsoever thou shalt loose on earth shall be loosed in heaven.

Although Jesus is referred to as the Rock in I Corinthians 10:4, neither His identity nor the rock-like aspect of His character is meant in this discourse to Peter. The thought Jesus is showing to Peter in these verses in Matthew is not about Himself as a rock, but the revelation from above - an example of which was just received by Peter - is to be the rock upon which the church is to be built. Jesus is talking about receiving revelation. It is upon revelation like this, like the revelation the Father just gave to Peter, that the Lord will build His church day in and day out.

You and I are not smart enough to figure out how to build His church! We need revelation to stay ahead of our very wily and evil enemy, satan[4]. Walking by the spirit is a walk by revelation, and this is how the Lord stated He would build His church.

John 15:5-8
*I am the vine, ye are the branches: He that abideth in me, and I in him, the same bringeth forth much fruit: **for without me ye can do nothing.***
If a man abide not in me, he is cast forth as a branch, and is withered; and men gather them, and cast them into the fire, and they are burned.
If ye abide in me, and my words [rhema, i.e. Jesus' revelation to you that comes as you spend time with Him at His table] ***abide in you***, *ye shall ask what ye will, and it shall be done unto you.*
Herein is my Father glorified, that ye bear much fruit; so shall ye be my disciples.

John 15:5 clearly states that without Jesus, we can do nothing. Not one thing can we do without Jesus. This means we can neither minister, nor build a work, heal, or operate any work for Him that will survive His fire unless it comes from Him in the first place. The manner in which information comes from Him is by revelation. As the old advertising slogan goes, "don't leave home without it." A church built by revelation day-by-day is a church against which the gates of hell will not prevail. I want a church like this. So do you. The revelation walk is how it comes about.

---

[4] *Ephesians 6:11-12*
Put on the whole armour of God, that ye may be able to stand against the wiles of the devil. For we wrestle not against flesh and blood, but against principalities, against powers, against the rulers of the darkness of this world, against spiritual wickedness in high places.

Tools for the Job
Matthew 16:19
And I will give unto thee the keys of the kingdom of heaven: and whatsoever thou shalt bind on earth shall be bound in heaven: and whatsoever thou shalt loose on earth shall be loosed in heaven.

Binding and loosing are part of the tool kit for building His church. The binding part refers both to binding ourselves *to* the things of God, as well as binding evil spirits, powers, and wicked spirits in high places *from* their evil operations. The loosing part of Matthew 16:19 refers to loosing strongholds of darkness, shattering, and destroying them.[iii] None of these can be effectively energized without first receiving revelation.

For example, who pushed back the fog in the previous chapter? Who pushed the water into a heap for the children of Israel to cross the Red Sea? Who dropped the walls of Jericho and who burned the captains and their 50 troops approaching to capture Elijah? All of these events and many others happened by revelation, spoken into being by a man or woman of God, and were carried out by the Holy Spirit or by angels.

You Can Walk By Revelation
God wants to give you revelation. The promise of John 14:12 is available to those who learn how to receive from God, and the New Testament clearly declares that God is no respector of persons.

John 14:10-13
Believest thou not that I am in the Father, and the Father in me? the words that I speak unto you I speak not of myself: but the Father that dwelleth in me, he doeth the works.

Believe me that I am in the Father, and the Father in me: or else believe me for the very works' sake.
Verily, verily, I say unto you, He that believeth on me, the works that I do shall he do also; and greater works than these shall he do; because I go unto my Father.
And whatsoever ye shall ask in my name, that will I do, that the Father may be glorified in the Son.

Verse 10 speaks of the words that the Father spoke to Jesus, who then turned around and delivered them to the disciples. This is how the Lord works with us! Ananias in Acts 9 is a perfect example of how this revelation thing works. Ananias was at home, perhaps in prayer, when the Lord told him to go witness to Saul, a feared Christian killer at that time.

In Acts 9:13-14, Ananias had a little trouble with this revelation, and told the Lord so. But Ananias had built a relationship with the Lord. He had confidence in the revelation that the Lord gave him (built by spending time alone with the Lord like you would do with any best friend). Though he had questions regarding his assignment, his hesitation to obey was relatively minor considering how potentially dangerous the task sounded.

John 10:27
My sheep hear my voice, and I know them, and they follow me:

Ananias was one of the flock. He was a sheep. He learned the sound of his Master's voice. If we want to be part of the flock, we must also learn to hear the sound of His voice.

Performing the Works of Jesus by Revelation
It is by the process of learning to hear His voice that we will receive the revelation necessary to not only do the works that Jesus did, but even greater works as mentioned in John 14:12.

Blasphemy you say? Impossible? After all Jesus is the son of God, and you and I are just mere men and women? These things died out with the apostles? Let's not choose to stay in the fog. The blasphemy is the failure to believe what is written in God's word. The blasphemy is in never learning to hear His voice and learning to obey it in order to walk in the power of an unchanging God. The blasphemy is in refusing to get out of the boat and walking toward Jesus on the water when He tells us to come.

Revelation is not for the "specially gifted". There is no such thing in the eyes of the Lord because He is no respector of persons. The manifestations of holy spirit are for every man to profit according to I Corinthians 12:7, and the profits are then listed in verses 8 through 10. "For to one" and "To another" are more accurately translated "For for one" and "for another", meaning for one and for another profit, not for one person or another person.

For years we have been held back by "gift" theology. But *the* gift referred to in these verses (not the gift ministries of Ephesians 4:12) is the gift from the Holy Spirit. And this particular gift of holy spirit[iv] has nine manifestations. I like to call them tools from the Holy Spirit's tool kit. Each one of the nine comes with the Holy Spirit's package (your holy spirit) that was received with the new birth, and each believer has the ability to use each one of the nine if they so desire. As in your house powered by electricity, the one source (Holy Spirit) energizes your holy spirit (the lights, radio, stove, dishwasher, etc.). In the case of speaking in tongues, your faith action is to move your lips and tongue. The Holy Spirit honors that faith by supplying the words. Hence it is the individual's responsibility to use what the Holy Spirit freely gives, and He supplies every time you elect to use it. Others of the nine manifestations of I Corinthians 12 often work this way as well. There is a mutual nature to the operation of the manifestations of the Holy Spirit.

Our Job Is Faith
Faith includes the free acceptance of the gift given by the Holy Spirit. Each individual who desires to speak in tongues, for example, must determine to meet the Holy Spirit halfway with enough faith to move their lips and tongue, and supply air through the vocal cords. Deciding to step out in faith to do these things is as important as getting rid of special gift thinking.

You are always in charge of your own free will because God, unlike the devil, never possesses or controls you. Ask anyone who speaks in tongues already. Can they start and stop anytime they want? Can they sing, shout, or whisper in tongues? Yes. God never oversteps a person's free will. To do so would violate God's unchanging laws. Once a person is born again, he or she governs whether and when they are going to speak in tongues by trusting the Holy Spirit that He has already given His spirit to do so, and then moving their own lips and mouth in faith.[v]

The Spirit divides to every man severally, both as the man wills (verse 11, check the antecedents), and as the Spirit wills. The will of the Holy Spirit is that all of God's children walk like Jesus Christ did with the same measure of holy spirit that He had!

In spite of all this, the Holy Spirit is able to go beyond the operation of these nine manifestations into special anointings.

Special Anointings From the Holy Spirit

The receipt of additional special anointings beyond the nine manifestations does not at all negate the Scripture regarding God being no respector of persons, for God has no respect of persons regarding every *invitation* of His written Word. But He can choose to go beyond His written Word any time He desires.

Confusion over the normal exercise of the nine manifestations of holy spirit (which arise from the package received when a person is born again), with special anointings[vi] from the Holy Spirit occurs frequently in Christian understanding. But such special anointings which go beyond the nine manifestations are strictly the prerogative of the Holy Spirit.

To illustrate, consider the healing ministry of Oral Roberts, Benny Hinn, Kathryn Kuhlman, John G. Lake, Smith Wigglesworth or any number of Christians who not only have operated the normal nine manifestations of holy spirit (speaking in tongues, tongues with interpretation, prophesy, word of knowledge, word of wisdom, discerning of spirits, faith, miracles and healing) but who also have evidenced an additional special gift anointing of healing. Praise God for this blessing to the Body of Christ! Consider the healing shadow of Peter in Acts 5:15, and the extraordinary healings from anointed aprons and handkerchiefs at the hands of Paul.

The point is that the gift of holy spirit in every believer has nine usual evidences which are fully available to each born again believer. Beyond these, the Holy Spirit has anointed individuals in special ways (other than or in conjunction with the gift ministries of apostles, prophets, pastors, evangelists, prophets and teachers, etc.) for service within the Body of Christ.

Getting Rid of Special Gift Thinking

Jesus Christ is the way, the truth, and the life. We want to get to know the sound of His voice, not only because we love Him, but also because without Him we can do nothing. So if we desire to draw closer to our best friend and be imitators of Him, let's get rid of "special gift theology" and take some time to be alone with Him each day. He already has given all He can give to you, but He patiently waits for you to ask Him how to practically use what you have received spiritually. He is still the Master teacher, and words are how both He and every other spirit creation of God most often communicate.

Like the story of the ten talents, the Lord has freely given the Holy Spirit. Let us not be slack in failing to put those talents to work, or slacker still in constructing pharasaical theological arguments which resist the Holy Spirit's full welcome and trust in your heart, and partnership within your church. The Lord's church is getting built by those who spend time in two-way conversations with the Architect.

Remember: Spend time alone with the Lord regularly (how about daily?) to learn to hear His voice (revelation) to you. Don't get stuck in the special gift rut. God is no respecter of persons, and you really can do all the things that Jesus Christ did (and even greater things - John 14:12) as you learn to use the tools you have already received as a born again believer. (By the way, if you are not born again, what are you waiting for? Read Romans 10:9 and ask Jesus to be your Lord. Make Him your Lord and lay your whole self at His feet. He'll figure out what needs to be done if you yield yourself to Him consistently, and take heed to what He tells you).

Chapter 3

The Antidote for the Lukewarm Church

Revelation chapter three contains staggering truths concerning how to remain on fire for the Lord, and how to grow more intimate with Him. Jesus is not someone who can't be touched. Not only is He a compassionate, loving, healing, powerful, and majestic Lord, but He is also a close friend. He has a sense of humor, and He is real. He deeply wants to become real to you. He wants to become your closest confidant, and like a mother or father loves to closely interact (and play!) with their children, so the Lord wants to closely interact with us. He wants us to learn to trust Him, and to enjoy being in close communication with Him.

In His revelation to the apostle John, Jesus also shows what is available for the believer who applies the principles contained therein. Let's take a look.

Revelation 3:20-22
*Behold, I stand at the door, and knock: **if any man hear my voice,** and open the door, I will come in to him, and will sup with him, and he with me.*
***To him that overcometh will I grant to sit with me in my throne,** even as I also overcame, and am set down with my Father in his throne.*
He that hath an ear, let him hear what the Spirit saith unto the churches.

This is Jesus talking to you and I. It is His message to the lukewarm church.[5] "Behold" means to pay attention, like we might say "Listen up!" The Lord wants us to pay attention to the fact that He is knocking and wants you to open the door. Why? So you can dine at His table. There's a turn in the tables once a person opens the door to Jesus. He comes in *your* door, but it's at *His* table that He invites you to dine! To "sup" in verse 20 means to eat, to dine. In context, it means to have an intimate fellowship around the table with Him.

Jesus is Always Knocking For Fellowship

How many times I have read this verse and thought it referred to a one-time event when I first became born again. But Jesus is knocking all the time! We need to eat everyday, and He knows that. When we eat at His table everyday, we are literally receiving manna from Him. Later on in Chapter Five, we'll see that this manna is referring to the receipt of revelation from the Lord. What a tremendous analogy He gave us through the apostle John to show the kind of relationship we are invited to have with Him!

In verse 21, Jesus states that to him that overcomes He will grant to sit with Him on His throne. Wow! What an incredible opportunity for us to enjoy, what a privilege it would be to sit with Him on His throne! Note the context – this privilege is extended to those who learn to dine with Him at His table. Dinner fellowship with Him at His table is the antidote to the

---

[5] *Revelation 3:14-16*
And unto the angel of the church of the Laodiceans write; These things saith the Amen, the faithful and true witness, the beginning of the creation of God; I know thy works, that thou art neither cold nor hot: I would thou wert cold or hot.
So then because thou art lukewarm, and neither cold nor hot, I will spue thee out of my mouth.

lukewarm church. Verse 22 underscores the importance of dining in intimate relationship with Him by saying if we have ears at all, pay attention to this message. It is what the Spirit is telling the churches. This message is for the entire church of Jesus Christ. It is for each member of the body of Christ. That means it is for you and I – *if* we elect to dine at His table, which happens *if* we elect to open the door. And He is always knocking.

Dinner Conversation
Now, let's talk about what happens at dinner. We eat food to get nourishment. We also eat food to socialize with close friends and family. God designed us to be both physically and mentally blessed by the breaking of bread together. Jesus expanded these benefits into the spiritual realm. He added at least two more blessings of His own. When a person dines with Him, they not only draw closer in friendship, fellowship and trust with Him (which sure does wonders for one's spiritual strength and confidence), but He also shares His heart. In so doing, He provides the revelation that we need to function for the day.

Let's back up a verse and ask a logical question. In verse 19, it says that whom Jesus loves, He rebukes and chastens. How does He do this? The answer is simple. He does it most often with words. Words are the instruments of spiritual power. Words are one of the primary means through which spiritual power is transmitted. We, as believers in Christ who are part of His body, appropriate the authority Jesus gave us via words. Every spirit being speaks in words. Jesus speaks in words. Both the Father and the Holy Spirit speak in words. People speak in words. Angels and fallen angels (demons, i.e. evil spirits) speak words. Words can build faith (Romans 10:17) and they can bewitch and enslave (Acts 8:5-13).

Let me illustrate. When God created the heavens and the earth, how did He do it? He spoke it into being with words. When a Christian casts out a demon, or ministers healing to another person, they use words, i.e. commands into the spirit realm. It is an awesome privilege and responsibility to have a mouth to speak words to which either angels or demons respond.

Angels are ministering spirits sent to minister to those who are the heirs of salvation according to Hebrews 1:14. Their response includes carrying out the words of faith spoken by believers. Demons do the opposite, responding to the curses uttered by people (including believers). Words of cursing often give legal authority for demons to further the work of satan. As instruments of spiritual power, words therefore must be carefully issued, and every idle word (*argos,* meaning unemployed, lazy, useless, barren, hollow, injurious[vii]) will be judged on the day of judgment (Matthew 12:36). Christians must guard their tongues with the utmost of care.

How Does Jesus Rebuke and Chasten?
The Lord rebukes and chastens via words. But if the members of His body have not learned how to hear His voice, they will not be able to hear His rebuking and chastening. He can't get warning messages to the person who hasn't learned to hear. He can't help them learn His heart for them, nor give them the revelation they need to avoid falling into traps and snares in family, school, job, marriages, etc.

One might think, "But I thought God can do anything, even getting through to the hardest of hearts." Yes, but some things He chooses not to do. For example He chose to woo Israel for forty years in the wilderness rather than force them to come to Him. Israel failed to hear and respond. The entire generation of people who were miraculously delivered from Egypt hardened their hearts against God and His voice. God's method has not changed since. He wants us to hear His voice and harden not our hearts just like He wanted for Israel (Hebrews 3:14-15; 4:6-7). Let us come in from our wilderness by learning to soften our hearts through hearing the Lord's voice each day.

Learning How to Hear Spiritual Words
A big key to learning how to hear is in the last part of verse 19.

Revelation 3:19
As many as I love, I rebuke and chasten: be zealous therefore, and repent.

We are to be zealous to repent. Repentance is not as simple as saying, "I'm sorry." To repent involves changing direction, not only to avoid repeating the mistake, but correcting it's consequences wherever possible. It requires a full change of the heart, motives, intentions, and actions. For example, a person might commit a grievous error in a marriage and the marriage turns bitterly into divorce. One spouse repents and genuinely changes heart. The other may also echo the same words but still refuse to let go of internal bitterness. That person may mouth forgiveness, but still refuses to take their spouse back. Which one has actually repented?

The entry requirement for fellowship around Jesus' table is to be zealous to change, to repent. This is a matter of the heart, not the larynx. And those whose hearts cannot hear, won't hear Jesus. He loves everybody. I love lots of people too. But I don't dine with all of them and neither does Jesus. We are not talking about love, we are talking about intimate dinner conversations of the heart with the Master. The ones whom He can fellowship with on an intimate level are the ones whose hearts are clean in repentance, and who elect to open the door to

His knock. We need food every day, so you can easily imagine how often Jesus knocks – about constantly!

The believers who overcome in this area of maintaining a lifestyle of repentance and seeking to dine at His table will be those whom He invites to sit at his throne. These are the folks who are not lukewarm. Let him who hath an ear hear what the Spirit says to the churches.

Drawing Closer to Him

Let's go a little further. But before we do, understand that the Lord loves you so much that if you were the only person who would ever come to Him, He would still have died for you with just as much joy in his heart. Yes, it was with great joy that He died for you (Hebrews 12:1-3), and He has also numbered every hair upon your head (Luke 12:7). His love for you is as particular and unique to you as you are particular and unique in the Body of Christ.

In Psalms 139 it says He is acquainted with all our ways, and knows our downsitting and our uprising. He knows our thoughts afar off – and still He loves us! He accepts us just the way we are right now. A big reason why He chastens and rebukes is to help us be able to draw closer to Him.

The Lord Jesus Christ loves you. He wants to spend time with you in His sanctuary, in His presence. He loves *you* personally, and He longs for you to get to know and have an active relationship with Him, one that is far better than your best earthly friend.

At the same time, let's get sober about drawing close to Him. There are no strings attached to the free gift of God. However, there are conditions. The conditions include the fact that He is not going to do your job for you. When Jesus comes back in judgment, and says to the world, "Why did you deliberately choose to avoid getting to know me personally and intimately while you had the free opportunity?", there will be no excuses accepted. His is the message of Isaiah, quoted also in Romans 10:21.

Isaiah 65:2
I have spread out my hands all the day unto a rebellious people, which walketh in a way that was not good, after their own thoughts;

The condition associated with being invited to sit with Jesus on His throne is not special favoritism. God the Father is no respector of persons (Acts 10:34) and neither is the Lord. But He does respect conditions – conditions of obedience to His written Word *and* conditions of obedience to His specific revelation into your heart, garnered from His dinner table.

Relationship is Everything
The specific condition noted in Revelation 3:21 is summarized in one word - relationship. Have you cultivated a relationship with The Lord? Is it an active two-way communication, a friendship built upon frequently spending time alone with Him?

Matthew 7:21-23
Not every one that saith unto me, Lord, Lord, shall enter into the kingdom of heaven; but he that doeth the will of my Father which is in heaven.
Many will say to me in that day, Lord, Lord, have we not prophesied in thy name? and in thy name have cast out devils? and in thy name done many wonderful works?
And then will I profess unto them, I never knew you: depart from me, ye that work iniquity.

Even those who regularly operate the nine manifestations of holy spirit, a prophetic or some other office in the church, can fail to actively know Jesus. If their revelation is not coming from Him, if they are not feeding from His table to get the revelation manna they need to function in His name, Jesus will rightfully say, "I never knew you". The word "know" in Matthew 7:23 literally means to know by experience. When He says "I never knew you", it means "I never had a personal, close relationship with you".

Confessing Jesus as Lord once *does* mean salvation as far as I know at this time from Romans 10:9 and 10. It does mean passing the entrance requirement in order to be a part of the new heavens and new earth for all eternity. But it does not mean a close relationship has been established. To build the kind of relationship with Jesus that results in a seat at His throne requires dining at His table daily – not just snacking! Just like we build relationships with friends on earth by spending lots of time together, so it is with building a close friendship with Jesus. We must make our day revolve around our appointments with Him, not force our time with Him to become cut short or non-existent.

"Depart from me ye that work iniquity". Workers of iniquity include Christians with works done in His name, but not at His direction. The word "iniquity" means lawlessness. To be lawless concerning our relationship with Jesus is to do things our own way rather than Jesus' way – the way He is willing to tell us if we took the time to ask. Revelation is how Jesus said He would build His church (see Chapter 2). But believers who fail to dine at the Master's table to get their daily marching orders often wind up entangled in *their own* religious activities (including trying to solve the problems of others) instead of the Lord's.

Like the surprised believers of Matthew 7 who even prophesied and cast out demons in His name but with whom the Lord will not know by an experiential relationship, we must take care to spend time with Him in His presence around His table. Revelation-less actions will become worthless fuel for His fire. Cain found this out the hard way. Let's obey like Abel, not Cain.

These are hard words. But they are not as hard as the judgment seat of Christ for those who spurn or neglect the opportunity to get to know Him in an intimate, personal relationship now.

"Behold I stand at the door and knock." Will you open the door of your heart each day to Him? Will you take the time to sit with Him at His table so He can share His heart with you? Will you take His yoke upon you to obey the things He will share with you to do? Best friends only love and want what is best for each other. Spend time with your best friend each day, and stay to eat the full meal, not just the appetizer. You will be astonished at the things He will tell you!

Learning to be Faithful
I wish I had learned to be faithful about dining daily with the Lord the first time He told me to. One noon time I was walking to lunch down a wide sidewalk while in seminary training. I had transferred from active navy duty to the reserves, and entered the seminary together with my wife, Rita. Two months into our three years of school, the Lord stopped me on the sidewalk to say that if I would take the time to talk with Him every day, it would change my life and my ministry. He wasn't talking about prayer time. He was talking about getting alone with Him and allowing Him to talk openly and intimately with me.

Sixteen years elapsed before I finally put this into daily practice. Although I did spend time in prayer *to* Him daily, my fellowship and listening time *with* Him, listening to what He wanted to say, was only sporadic during any given week. Looking back now, I see that although He shared what He could in the time I allotted to Him, it took me sixteen years before I finally committed myself to faithfully and literally carry out the "dining" instructions He gave me that day on the sidewalk. Again, I'm not talking about times of talking *to* Him in prayer. I'm referring to taking the time to talk *with* Him, spending most of the time listening to His response, and doing it daily.

Two years after graduating from the seminary I became a full time minister, and traveled extensively around the world teaching the Bible. But as can happen when we fail to stay close enough to the lips of the Lord, burn out set in after about eight years. Mind you, I was still very actively teaching the Bible and doing all the religious (but revelation-less) things I was used to doing. I moved to another state to start some home church fellowships. To support my family I went to work as a manufacturing facilities engineer. Eventually I became an engineering manager for a division of a Fortune 200 company. The Lord healed me and my family, and taught me again about humility before Him. But I didn't make it easy.

One day the Lord told me to leave the naval reserve. I was a full commander by this time, an O-5. It took three years for me to obey because I liked the service. But He told me this was his third and final warning. I obeyed and resigned my commission of 17 years. I realize now this was needful because the relatively senior position was a stronghold of pride for me. Pride kills intimacy with the Lord quicker than you can spell the word.

A few more years elapsed, and I took a class on how to exercise our spiritual authority. I learned to know Jesus personally instead of just intellectually. And then one day while teaching a teen Bible camp, the Lord told me that if I would make a vow to worship and praise Him every day, and spend time each day with Him in His presence, He would change my life, and cause my ministry to rise out of obscurity and become a part of His plan for the close of the age. I was already on my knees when He spoke these words into my spirit. I vowed to spend time with Him each day in praise and worship as tears flowed from my eyes. His grace is staggering, and I am so grateful to Him for patiently teaching me to serve Him first before I steam ahead smartly trying to serve others.

It has been two years since this day. I learned the difference between snacking and dining at His table. I found myself more than once lying exhausted in bed after a typically long 12 hour day in the office, suddenly remembering I hadn't praised and worshipped yet. But, faithful to fulfill my vow, I would get out of bed and onto my knees to praise and worship Him, confess my sins, and spend time honoring Him with sacrifices of praise.

The "Sound" of Revelation
An interesting thing started to happen. Sometimes I would minister to the Lord for ten or fifteen minutes before I became aware that the Lord wanted to share His heart with me. From deep within my spirit, He would "speak", not words I heard with my ears, but words which would ordinarily be easily construed as my own thoughts – except they weren't. It was almost as if it was my same inner thought "voice", but the thoughts were not originating from me, and they came from deep down within me, not from my head.

This is a difficult point for most people to overcome because demons and our own souls are so ready to tell us that words like these are simply originating from our own thoughts. But a strong Scriptural knowledge enables God's people to recognize thoughts and revelation which are in harmony with the written Word, and also recognize those thoughts and revelation which conflict with the written Word. The written Word is the most important check and balance, and will never conflict with revelation received from the Lord.

In addition, there is an inward witness in the spirit[6] which will confirm spiritual truth, whether it comes in the form of prophecy, or into your holy spirit within. The mere content of the words Jesus speaks into your spirit will be wholly different than you could even think up on your own. But the "voice" comes through your own self from deep within your spirit,[7] and has to ultimately transmit into your brain through the same collection of brain cells that your own thoughts utilize. Hence words from the Lord often have a similar "tone of voice" as your own thoughts, and are harder to distinguish than if the

---

[6] *Romans 8:16 - The Spirit itself beareth witness with our spirit, that we are the children of God:*
I John 3:24 - And he that keepeth his commandments dwelleth in him, and he in him. And hereby we know that he abideth in us, by the Spirit which he hath given us.
I John 4:13 - Hereby know we that we dwell in him, and he in us, because he hath given us of his Spirit.

[7] *John 7:37-39 - In the last day, that great day of the feast, Jesus stood and cried, saying, If any man thirst, let him come unto me, and drink.*
He that believeth on me, as the scripture hath said, out of his belly shall flow rivers of living water.
(But this spake he of the Spirit, which they that believe on him should receive: for the Holy Ghost was not yet given; because that Jesus was not yet glorified.)

same words came from another person sitting next to you. Elijah heard it as a "still small voice", and this is as good a description as you'll ever find.

The Lord's still small voice will sound different to you than it does to me. **But it will never contradict the written Word of God, and it will always be confirmed by the inward spiritual witness within you**. These two are your check and balance. The Lord will work with you individually to teach you how to hear His voice. He's the One that wants you to hear it!

Often Christians try too hard to get their experiences to match the experiences of others, especially in this area of hearing the Lord talk with them. I advise believers to forget about their desires and simply enjoy praising and worshipping the Lord. He will talk when He is ready, and He'll do it when we have surrendered our intellectual pride to Him about the way we think He ought to work. The Lord can't get through a noisy brain that is full of anxiety. He's pleased to listen to your problems, but problem pray-ers are not often victory praisers! He's pleased to listen to our honest questions, but not our intellectually religious doctrines any more than He was pleased to listen to the know-it-all Pharisees. Letting the Lord communicate with us is based on trust, not on our own doctrine.

Psalm 100 tells us to enter His gates with thanksgiving and His courts with praise, not kick at the gates with anxiety and stumble on the steps with burdens and unbelief. If we intellectually disallow the Spirit of the Lord from talking to us around the hearthfire of His heart, how will we ever get to know Him personally? You don't know me personally by the book I write, though intellectually you know much about me. We come to know and build a relationship with another person by talking to them and hearing them talk back. We know and build a relationship with the Lord in person the same way. If all we can proclaim is that we had an intellectual knowledge of the Lord on the day of judgment, then the message of Matthew 7 is that we will sadly learn we were lawlessly sacrificing like Cain instead of being led by His Spirit to sacrifice like Abel.

Satan's Counterfeit

People who don't know the voice of the Lord often declare that every demon-possessed killer hears voices, implying that anyone who does hear an inner voice is equally as prone to bizarre acts. So let's take a moment to think about how the devil works.

Words are instruments of power. The devil has to use the same instruments God invented in order to exercise spiritual power. The devil doesn't have his own physical body – only humans have physical bodies. So in order to exercise spiritual power, he's got to get human agents to do his work for Him. The devil can't do anything that is original. If he could, he wouldn't have to steal, kill and destroy to try to get enough of what he wants.[8]

All originality comes from the one true God. For example, Proverbs 8:12 declares that God is the source of all knowledge and discretion, the source of all witty inventions. Satan works long and hard to get people (both believers and unbelievers) to yield their will to him in order to gain legal access into their bodies and souls to continue his thievery. How many Christians have had their health, finances, or family relationships stolen from them? Is this because they are exclusively at fault, or have they unwittingly admitted the thief into their lives? Few do this

---

[8] *John 10:10 - The thief cometh not, but for to steal, and to kill, and to destroy: I am come that they might have life, and that they might have it more abundantly.*

willingly or totally. But satan tricks people into willful sin in order to gain legal access.

Satan delights in getting *Christians* to participate in his works. Believers yield their will to him in perhaps seemingly small ways. Have you never seen a fellow believer caught in unforgiveness, bitterness, and resentment? What doors these open to demonic attack! The very fact that some Christians today believe they cannot become demonized (at least in part) by demons through this will-yielding process is indicative of satan's subtlety in manipulating Christian doctrine.

Once yielded by free will of the person, satan tries to enlarge his beachhead through weak points in a person's spiritual armor. Holes of unyielded flesh such as lust, attitudes born from wrong beliefs, physical dependencies, etc. grow if unattended in repentance. It is a special treasure to satan if he can get political and religious heads to yield their will to him because of the influence they exert. Once a person yields enough portions of his or her free will, a demon can possess, control, or influence some or many of their physical and mental actions.[viii]

God's Way is Different

God *never* possesses or controls. He will never overstep free will. Jesus never takes control of anyone's body or mind – any more than your best friend would ever do so. God never forces Himself on anyone. But that doesn't mean the Lord doesn't invite people to freely and willfully accept His invitation to come into His presence and dine with Him. The choice is always up to the individual. Whether they elect to ignore this invitation, or undermine it with ridiculous comparisons to satan's practices or not, the Lord is still the Lord. His ways are higher than our ways, and man's contrary, prideful, and religiously intellectual opinions otherwise don't change the Lord's offer.

God will not change the way He chooses to conduct business with His people. If we don't want to spend time alone with the Lord every day, that's our choice. If we want to dine with Him, but don't feel like praising and worshipping our way into the front hallway, that's entirely up to us. But narrow is His way,[9] and He is not going to change it. First Peter 5:5 clearly declares that God resists the proud, but gives grace to the humble.[10] The opportunity to dine with Him each day is great mercy, and a privilege never to be taken lightly.

Growing to be God-Reliant
Sometimes the Lord has so much to say that the moment I drop to my knees, He starts speaking. Always I have noticed that He is more ready to speak than I am to listen. In teaching the Bible, and ministering healing to people, I have learned that by relying on Him to set the agenda for the day, the results are amazing.

After about a month of faithfully spending time dining with Him each day (whether it was near midnight or not!), the Lord told me He wanted to lead me into different pastures than I was used to. He said these pastures would be places where the grass isn't as green with Bible knowledge, where the fences needed mending, and where there were big stones that needed to be

---

[9] *Matthew 7:14 - Because strait is the gate, and narrow is the way, which leadeth unto life, and few there be that find it.*

[10] *1 Peter 5:5 - Likewise, ye younger, submit yourselves unto the elder. Yea, all of you be subject one to another, and be clothed with humility: for God resisteth the proud, and giveth grace to the humble.*

pulled out. Within that week I was led to disband our home church, and visit another nearby church.

A month or two later the Lord directed me to begin making plans to minister in India. I arranged to take three weeks of vacation from my company and joined a team of 26 other ministers. We ministered in villages and cities, big churches and small home fellowships. The Lord won people who had never heard the gospel of Jesus at each place, sometimes hundreds at a time! Dramatic physical healings took place.

During this trip the Lord woke me up early one morning and told me He would begin teaching me the principles of spiritual warfare contained in the book of Joshua, and teach the entire book to me verse by verse. I can state unequivocally that Jesus sure knows the Bible! When you ask the Lord to teach you His Word, you are in for some great spiritual learning indeed. What He taught me is amazing. What he will teach you will be equally amazing!

At that time He told me he would remove the shackles of secular work from my feet, that He was calling me to return to full-time ministry. I was delighted, but not without some trepidation.

How would I pay my mortgage and other debts? I repented for being in debt, but nevertheless, there I was. The very day I returned home from India, the elders of our new church asked me if I would assume duties as Pastor. When I asked the Lord, He quickly told me "Yes, as long as you lead people to me." This I was very glad to do.

Six months went by. The Lord told me He wanted me to go on a trip to Romania to minister to God's people there. In order to go, I knew I would have to quit working my secular job. Will the Lord really take care of me? I wasn't fond of 12 hour work days, but executive positions pay good salaries. But the Lord assured me that He would be a better employer than my corporation, and that my salary would grow, not decline. I had no cash reserves. But as I continue spending time with the Lord dining at His table, He continues to raise me up as a more serviceable vessel for Him, and our bills are getting paid.

To do this, He had to help me grow God-reliant instead of corporation job-reliant. Does He need to do it this way with everyone? No. His curriculum is different for each one of us. It has to be different for two reasons. First, none of us are perfect like Jesus Christ. Hence, by sheer necessity, each member of the body has different needs and only Jesus can figure out how to supply them properly. Secondly, no single person has the "all truth" that Jesus has. Each one of us has some truth, but Jesus has it all. And His individualized curriculum provides for our inability to learn everything at once.

Jesus Has A Special Curriculum For You
Jesus may teach things to one person, regardless of their spiritual maturity, that you or I may not know. Perhaps the only way we will learn them is from that person. But if that person fails to learn what Jesus wants to teach them, we might never get the benefit of that learning. My point is this: we all need each other in the body. No one individual is dispensable. No one is more important, and we need each other desperately!

So now I am once again working for the Lord full time. Each day I depend on the Lord to pay my salary and do the normal things any employer is supposed to do. As His employee, I check in with Him each morning to learn what he wants me to do for the day. My first two weeks went like this:

The first day back home from Romania, the Lord told me to make that day a praise day. So all day long I praised Him and did praise-related activities such as transcribing praise songs to be used in the church, researched praise verses from Psalms, etc.

The second day, He told me I could do anything I wanted, and that it would be a day of great rejoicing. I had the sense it would involve finances because I was mildly anxious about post-trip bills. I worked in my office that day until noon, and did some work around the house after that. By early evening I was done – jet lag was catching up to me. My son brought in the mail to me, and in the mail was a letter with a lovely note from a believer I hadn't heard from in over a year. He also sent a large donation check. I rejoiced at the Lord's amazing confirmation of His care for me and my family. Each day that week I received donations in the mail.

Day three was even more fun. The Lord told me He would send me out to do a miracle. I was led by the Lord to visit a friend whose emergency surgery had never healed in five years. The doctors couldn't figure out why. But by claiming his healing in the name of Jesus Christ, and by removing the curses that have plagued his life, he is healing rapidly. His progress has been amazing.

A day or two later the Lord told me to minister to a family. I wound up ministering healing to not only that family, but also to their parents, and later that evening to a couple I met while on an errand at a department store!

Great Faith Comes from Great Relationship
The point is this: as noted previously in Chapter 2, the Lord will build His church by revelation. He gives revelation to those who hear his voice. Although He may give revelation to others who don't spend time dining at His table, there will be a remarkable difference in its quantity, consistency, and caliber. There is a big difference between keeping appointments with the Teacher, spending the time necessary to get regular full lessons, vs. failing to keep appointments or playing telephone tag for so long that the lesson is never taught.

Hearing His voice is developed by spending time with Him. He may reveal Himself to different believers differently, i.e. perhaps through visions, an audible voice as opposed to an inner voice, etc. He nevertheless *will* reveal Himself. Jesus died so that you could have a permanent and lasting interactive relationship with the Godhead.

Not one of the great men and women mentioned in Hebrews chapter 11 were any different than you, except you have more Bible to believe, and more resources from Jesus to work with. The great part about each of our Hebrews 11 forefathers was not that they had faith. The great part was *the basis* of their faith - an active personal *relationship* with the Lord. They were so confident of His voice when He spoke into their spirit, and therefore so trusting of it when they heard it, that they had no doubts about obeying it! We can each learn to do the same.

Remember: Great revelation yields great faith. But great revelation is preceded by a great relationship with the Lord. And our relationship with the Lord becomes great when we dine at the Master's table daily. This is the antidote to being lukewarm. He wants us to be zealous to repent, and have our ears close to His lips.

Chapter 4

Abiding in Him: How to Check Your Pulse

John 14:10
Believest thou not that I am in the Father, and the Father in me? the words [rhema] *that I speak unto you I speak not of myself: but the Father that dwelleth in me, he doeth the works.*

Jesus Christ declared that the words He spoke to the disciples were words that our Father spoke to Him. These are revelation words from God, and they model how both Jesus and our Father continue to communicate to us today. God communicated to Jesus Christ in words. Those words came into Jesus' spirit the same way He gives words into the spirit of believers today. Let's look at this word "word" more closely.

The translation for "word" in verse 10 is the Greek word *rhema.* There are other Greek words translated the same way in our English Bibles. Notably among them is the word *logos.* A *logos* is a communication from the Father. A *logos* can be written, spoken, a vision, etc. *Logos* simply means communication. Jesus is called the *Logos* in John chapter 1. A *rhema*, on the other hand, is a specific oral communication. It is an inspired utterance. Often when referring to specific revelation given to an individual, the Scriptures use the word *rhema.* Here in verse 10, Jesus is saying that the words of revelation that the Father gave Him, He passed on to the disciples. Jesus' entire ministry was by revelation spoken to people. As noted in chapter two, this is the way He builds His church.

John 3:31-34
He that cometh from above is above all: he that is of the earth is earthly, and speaketh of the earth: he that cometh from heaven is above all.
And what he hath seen and heard, that he testifieth; and no man receiveth his testimony.
He that hath received his testimony hath set to his seal that God is true.
For he whom God hath sent speaketh the words [rhema] **of God:** *for God giveth not the Spirit by measure unto him.*

Miracles from *Rhema*

God sent Jesus to speak revelation words. Jesus is sending us to speak words too – words of revelation, *rhema*-powered words from above. The reason why Jesus could do miracles then is the same reason why we can do them today – He received revelation from the Father. When He spoke these words, miracles were energized. It's no different with every miracle in the Bible. Miracles are done of men and women by first receiving revelation, and when the revelation is obeyed and carried out, the miracle is energized into physical reality by God. In chapter 7, this topic is shown more clearly in the study of Hebrews.

The more time we spend in worship and praise alone with the Lord, the more we dine at His table, the more revelation we will receive. Hence, the more miracles we will do. For example, where was Peter when the Lord gave him the revelation to go to Cornelius' house? Peter was on a rooftop praying. What was Cornelius doing? He is noted as a devout man in Acts 10:2 who prayed always. The revelation they received moved the Gospel out of its Jerusalem center and into the Gentile world.

No one can deny the impact that the written Word has had on Christianity. Today, people (generally those who don't get much revelation) often minimize, or even disparage the thought that *rhema* words are essential to the Christian walk. There should be, and indeed there can be, no contradiction between revelation received and written Scripture if the revelation received is from the Lord. The written Word must always validate the *rhema* received.

It is important to recognize that most of the early first century church did not have the Pauline revelation or the written Gospels to guide them. What then did they have after Jesus was crucified? They had what we are supposed to have – a daily telephone line connected to the Lord.

John 15:7-8
If ye abide in me, and my words [rhemata] *abide in you, ye shall ask what ye will, and it shall be done unto you.*
Herein is my Father glorified, that ye bear much fruit; so shall ye be my disciples.

How is God glorified and how is the fruit borne? All spiritual fruit comes from the strength of the spiritual vine. Jesus is the vine and we are the branches. A branch needs nourishment daily, and so do we. Many Christians may be weak branches because they don't eat sufficiently at the Master's table. Therefore they fail to acquire the revelation, the *rhema*, needed to do the Lord's will for that day. The master of the vineyard must also prune out the unprofitable, weak branches, in order to produce better fruit.

John 15:1-3
I am the true vine, and my Father is the husbandman.
Every branch in me that beareth not fruit he taketh away: and
every branch that beareth fruit, he purgeth it, that it may
bring forth more fruit.
Now ye are clean through the word which I have spoken unto
you.
Abide in me, and I in you. As the branch cannot bear fruit of
itself, except it abide in the vine; no more can ye, except ye
abide in me.

How To Know When You Are Abiding in Jesus

There's a simple way to know if you are abiding in Him. Is He pruning your branch? Are you being led to clean up things in your life, are you being convicted to walk more closely with Him, and become more honest in your relationships with others? Or do you continue to make excuses and denials, hardening your heart to behavior, unforgiveness, resentment and bitterness that you know are wrong toward others who have hurt you?

The Lord is a man of war. He will not tolerate sin, and He won't tolerate our failure to deal with things He has already told us to fix. But when we take the time to privately fellowship with Him each day, we'll find His pruning is most often a gentle guidance, a compelling and supportive encouragement to help us grow more holy out of love for Him. If this pruning process is ongoing as a result of His leading in our lives, we can be assured that we are abiding in Him. The person who is zealous to repent, whom the Lord can chasten and rebuke via *rhema* words of revelation into his or her spirit, is the person whose branches He can prune.

John 15:5-6
I am the vine, ye are the branches: He that abideth in me, and I
*in him, the same bringeth forth much fruit: **for without me ye***
can do nothing.
If a man abide not in me, he is cast forth as a branch, and is
withered; and men gather them, and cast them into the fire, and
they are burned.

A curse across all Christianity is the curse of trying to bring
forth fruit from self-inspired, Godly sounding works. Unless
your works are as a result of the Master's direction, they will be
burned. Self-directed works are nothing because they come
from nothing but religious pride. Carnal Christians are full of
do-gooding motivation which disgusts the Lord. Cain was a do-
gooder who was committed to do-good sacrifices. He became
angry when he found out the Lord cared nothing for them. But
like self-inspired Christians everywhere who look like they
mean well, Cain deliberately followed his own counsel instead
of the Lord's specific revelation. The whole point of Israel's 40
year wandering was to teach them to depend upon the Lord.

Many Christians today are still wandering. We must all learn to
eat from the Master's table or we will die in the do-gooder's
wilderness, and never see the victory of our promised land of
personal relationship with Jesus Christ.

John 15:7
*If ye abide in me, **and my words** [rhema] **abide in you**, ye shall*
ask what ye will, and it shall be done unto you.

If revelation from the Lord Jesus Christ is the manna for your
day, then His words are abiding in you. If you are hearing and
responding to revelation from Him, then it says in verse seven
that you are free to ask what you will, and it shall be done for

you. Verse seven is what I think of as a "whatsoever" verse, one of the "blank check" verses, such as "whatsoever ye shall ask in my name".[11] I used to read such verses and presume there were no stings attached. There aren't – for those who have learned to faithfully dine at His table, learning to hear and do His *rhema*. *If ye abide in me, and* [if] *my words* [rhema] *abide in you, ye shall ask what ye will, and it shall be done unto you.*

Friends Not Servants

As we learn to obey *rhema* instructions from the Lord, we make a transition in relationship. We become His friends instead of mere servants. Obedience to Jesus' direct revelation to individual believers is the criteria which determines whether they become friends of Jesus, or merely servants.

John 15:14-16
Ye are my friends, if ye do whatsoever I command you.
Henceforth I call you not servants; *for the servant knoweth not what his lord doeth:* ***but I have called you friends;*** *for all things that I have heard of my Father I have made known unto you.*
Ye have not chosen me, but I have chosen you, and ordained you, that ye should go and bring forth fruit, and that your fruit should remain: that whatsoever ye shall ask of the Father in my name, he may give it you.

Fullness of joy is found in being a friend of Jesus! What fun it is to laugh and talk over deep things of the heart together! Friends share their innermost secrets, and they trust one another with their lives. As we grow into an intimate relationship with Jesus through spending time alone with Him each day, we shift from a servant relationship to one of friendship. A committed

---

[11] Matthew 18:19; 21:22; Mark 11:24; John 14:13&14; 15:16; 16:23; I John 3:22; 5:14&15.

friend is higher than a servant, yet a friend will still faithfully carry out the servant's work asked by a friend. The revelation walk with the Lord is a walk of friendship in obedience.

Remember: Without the direct revelation from Jesus Christ, we can do nothing.[12] All our own works, even the ones that seem like great ideas, will be burned. We receive more revelation as we spend time alone with Him and develop a close friendship with the Master teacher. He will purge and prune us so that we can glorify the Father. Let Him prune you so that your branch can bring forth more fruit for Him.

---

[12] *John 15:5 - I am the vine, ye are the branches: He that abideth in me, and I in him, the same bringeth forth much fruit: for without me ye can do nothing.*

SECTION II

Eating Manna From The Lord's Table

Chapter 5

Would You Like Some More Manna, Son?

Jesus Christ is still knocking on the door of our heart to dine with us. We know from Deuteronomy 6 and Mark 12 that we are to love the Lord our God with all our heart, soul, mind and strength, and from John 14:23 that we express this love by keeping His words. From John 15:4-6 we further know that without abiding continually in Jesus, the Vine, we can do nothing, and our self-inspired works of nothing are cast into the fire.

In contrast, verse 15:7 says that as we abide in Him by allowing His *rhema* (inspired revelation words) to abide in us, fruit is produced that glorifies the Father. Rhema words are gathered from personal conversations with the Lord around His table. This is precisely the mechanism which the Lord indicated He would use to build His church in Matthew 16:13-18. We know also from John 5:38-40 when the Lord challenged the Pharisees to search for Him in the Scriptures, that an intellectual study of the Scriptures alone without knowing Jesus personally would not enable them to receive life.

How the Word of God was Written
It is helpful at this point to discover just how the written revelation of the Scriptures came to be written. We will see that the manner of hearing the Lord's voice mentioned thus far is

the same manner the Lord used to inspire men of God to write the Bible.

Revelation 1:1-5, 9-11
The Revelation of Jesus Christ, which God gave unto him, to shew unto his servants things which must shortly come to pass; and he sent and signified it by his angel unto his servant John:
Who bare record of the word of God, and of the testimony of Jesus Christ, and of all things that he saw.
Blessed is he that readeth, and they that hear the words of this prophecy, and keep those things which are written therein: for the time is at hand.
John to the seven churches which are in Asia: Grace be unto you, and peace, from him which is, and which was, and which is to come; and from the seven Spirits which are before his throne;
And from Jesus Christ, who is the faithful witness, and the first begotten of the dead, and the prince of the kings of the earth. Unto him that loved us, and washed us from our sins in his own blood,

I John, who also am your brother, and companion in tribulation, and in the kingdom and patience of Jesus Christ, was in the isle that is called Patmos, for the word of God, and for the testimony of Jesus Christ.
I was in the Spirit on the Lord's day, and heard behind me a great voice, as of a trumpet,
Saying, I am Alpha and Omega, the first and the last: and,
What thou seest, write in a book, *and send it unto the seven churches which are in Asia; unto Ephesus, and unto Smyrna, and unto Pergamos, and unto Thyatira, and unto Sardis, and unto Philadelphia, and unto Laodicea.*

John 1 declares that Jesus is the Word. It should be no surprise that He gave the book of Revelation to John. Jesus got it from God. Each one communicated through words by the Spirit. Jesus instructed John (verses 9-11) to write what he was hearing by revelation into a book and send it to seven specific churches.

John was ministering, some say in exile, on the island of Patmos at the time, about 35 miles off the coast of modern day Turkey. John didn't question the silly details like, "How am I going to get this printed and mailed to these places once I even figure out how to find enough paper!" He just obeyed what the Lord told Him to do. In the second book of Peter we see how others responded to a similar leading of the Lord through the Holy Spirit, giving them revelation words:

2 Peter 1:20 and 21
Knowing this first, that no prophecy of the scripture is of any private interpretation.
For the prophecy came not in old time by the will of man: but holy men of God spake as they were moved by the Holy Ghost.

Prophecy and revelation both come by the same Spirit. It was the Holy Spirit, acting through His gift of holy spirit within John which moved him to write what Jesus dictated. This process is even more clearly seen in Paul's account in Galatians.

Galatians 1:11 and 12
*But I certify you, brethren, that **the gospel which was preached of me is not after man.***
*For I neither received it of man, neither was I taught it, **but by the revelation of Jesus Christ.***

Jesus Christ gave revelation to the church and charged it to be written down. There is only one author to the Bible – many scribes, but only one author. All of these scribes first learned to hear the voice of the Lord, and depend on it. They learned to carry out the instructions precisely as they were given. We need to do the same if we are going to play on His team and contribute *anything* to His church.

2 Timothy 3:16 and 17
All scripture is given by inspiration of God, *and is profitable for doctrine, for reproof, for correction, for instruction in righteousness:*
That the man of God may be perfect, throughly furnished unto all good works.

All Scripture comes by inspiration, i.e. revelation. The reason why 2 Peter 1:21 mentioned that it was *holy* men of God who were moved by the Holy Ghost is that no one sustains a consistent revelation walk with the Lord without consistent holiness. And no one can walk a holy life without faithfully "checking in" with Jesus and submitting to His active, revelation-giving voice.

How wonderfully and simply the Lord authored His written Word! With the same simplicity, He wants to communicate to each one of His children. His desire is to help us walk in the revelation walk of the Spirit and to produce fruit that glorifies Him. What a privilege we have today to so walk with our Lord and Savior, listen to His instructions, and carry out His plan to build His church!

Spiritual Meat
In Revelation 3:19[13] the Lord chastens and rebukes via words.

---

[13] *Revelation 3:19: As many as I love, I rebuke and chasten: be zealous therefore, and repent.*

In Revelation 3:20[14], the Lord fellowships around His table with those who hear His voice and open the door. In John 15:7[15], abiding in Him is equated with abiding in His *rhema* (word, an inspired utterance).

A *rhema* comes by way of an inner voice from the Lord. A *rhema* is revelation. Examples of such *rhema* include the inspired utterances from Jesus to John to write the book of Revelation (Revelation 1:1-19), from Jesus to Paul in Galatians 1:11 and 12 to preach (and subsequently write) the New Testament Scriptures. All of these terms – abide, dine, fellowship, chasten and rebuke – all involve an ongoing, conversational, interactive and deeply intimate relationship with the Lord Jesus Christ.

But Jesus didn't stop with only these terms to describe His point. He imported yet another illustration of the same idea – spiritual meat.

John 6:26-27
Jesus answered them and said, Verily, verily, I say unto you, Ye seek me, not because ye saw the miracles, but because ye did eat of the loaves, and were filled.
Labour not for the meat which perisheth, but for that meat which endureth unto everlasting life, *which the Son of man shall give unto you: for him hath God the Father sealed.*

---

[14] *Revelation 3:20: Behold, I stand at the door, and knock: if any man hear my voice, and open the door, I will come in to him, and will sup with him, and he with me.*
[15] *John 15:7: If ye abide in me, and my words* [rhema] *abide in you, ye shall ask what ye will, and it shall be done unto you.*

Jesus will give meat to His followers. What meat is this which endures all the way unto eternal life? It is the meat supplied at His table. It is revelation meat from Him.

Spiritual Manna

Attempting to switch to a subject they could better grapple with, the Pharisees asked a question in verse 28, "What shall we do, that we might work the works of God?" Jesus' answer was that they were to believe - have faith - in Himself as the Christ. They demanded a sign to prove His authenticity, such as the manna received during the wandering in the wilderness.

In mentioning the manna, the Pharisees mistakenly declared that Moses had given it to their ancestors. Jesus corrected them by saying that Moses didn't give them manna, but the Father. Jesus then added more details which came as *rhema* revelation from the Father. He called this manna not just bread from heaven, but true bread. He clearly stated that the bread from heaven is, in fact, the person whom God sent to give life to the world.

The Pharisees ignored the person part, and instead focused on the reference to bread and everlasting life. They asked, "Lord, evermore give us this bread." Jesus responded with a clear declaration:

John 6:35
*And Jesus said unto them, **I am the bread of life**: he that cometh to me shall never hunger; and he that believeth on me shall never thirst.*

Just as the manna sustained God's people during the wandering, so would the new manna, the Son of God, sustain God's people from this time forward. In Verse 47 Jesus returned to the bread topic, and described Himself as being manna from heaven.

Would You Like Some More Manna, Son?

John 6:47-51
*Verily, verily, I say unto you, **He that believeth on me hath
everlasting life.***
I am that bread of life.
Your fathers did eat manna in the wilderness, and are dead.
***This is the bread** which cometh down from heaven, that a man
may eat thereof, and not die.*
***I am the living bread** which came down from heaven: if any
man eat of this bread, he shall live for ever: **and the bread that
I will give is my flesh**, which I will give for the life of the world.*

Let's think about these verses in light of Matthew 4:4. We can
begin to see clearly the nature and function of the manna Jesus
is referencing.

Matthew 4:4
*But he answered and said, It is written, **Man shall not live by
bread alone, but by every word** [rhema] **that proceedeth out of
the mouth of God.***

Jesus is manna for us today. But how is He literally our
sustenance? He is our sustenance by the words [*rhema*] that He
provides to all who elect to dine at His table. Just as manna in
the wilderness was to be collected daily, so should we be
collecting His revelation daily at His table. Just as yesterday's
manna would rot on the ground, so will our use of yesterday's
revelation prove unfruitful for today's work for Him. Just as
our physical bodies need food to eat daily, so today are God's
people to live by depending on His revelation manna daily!

Give Us Our Daily Bread
Have you ever wondered why the phrase "give us our daily
bread" appears in the Lord's prayer? This prayer appears in
Matthew 6:7-13, and is a prayer for *spiritual* needs to be met.

Following the Lord's prayer, Jesus corrected the pharisaic practice of fasting publicly rather than secretly (Matthew 6:14-18). Jesus then focused on physical needs (Matthew 6:19-33). In so doing, He clearly switched from the *spiritual* focus of the Lord's prayer to a focus on the physical.

The remainder of Matthew chapter six is devoted to teaching dependence on God for *physical* needs – i.e. don't lay up treasures in earth, don't serve mammon, consider the lilies of the field and how they grow without toiling or spinning, and so on. The birds of the air neither sow nor reap, but God takes care of them. Don't be of little faith, He said, seeking after physical requirements like the Gentiles, but seek first the kingdom of God and His righteousness and all physical requirements will be met.

In contrast, the preceding verses consist of the Lord's prayer, which is focused on spiritual things. The prayer's reference to "give us our daily bread" is a request for spiritual sustenance (literally a "down upon sustenance" in the Greek), rather than being a request for physical food. As we have learned, spiritual bread is meant for our sustenance and specifically consists of revelation -- the spiritual manna we need each day to function and to build His church.

Clearly, Jesus is our Revelation Giver, *the* Bread that gives life. He is the One who said "The words [*rhema*] that I give unto you, they are spirit and they are life (John 6:63). He gives these words by providing revelation, and that revelation sustains us in our work for the kingdom.

Daily Feeding
Eating physical food is a daily function. Spiritual eating must be a daily function too. We eat spiritually through His

revelation manna. We get it from dining at His table, hearing inspired words from Him.

John 6:51-58
I am the living bread which came down from heaven: if any man eat of this bread, he shall live for ever: and the bread that I will give is my flesh, which I will give for the life of the world.
The Jews therefore strove among themselves, saying, How can this man give us his flesh to eat?
Then Jesus said unto them, Verily, verily, I say unto you, Except ye eat the flesh of the Son of man, and drink his blood, ye have no life in you.
Whoso eateth my flesh, and drinketh my blood, hath eternal life; and I will raise him up at the last day.
For my flesh is meat indeed, and my blood is drink indeed.
He that eateth my flesh, and drinketh my blood, dwelleth in me, and I in him.
As the living Father hath sent me, and I live by the Father: so he that eateth me, even he shall live by me.
This is that bread which came down from heaven: not as your fathers did eat manna, and are dead: he that eateth of this bread shall live for ever.

Nine Illustrations, One Truth
Verse 51 of John's Gospel elaborates further on the nature of this bread, declaring it also to be Jesus' flesh. Thus with a multitude of images used to describe a single spiritual reality, Jesus depicted the need for His daily revelation to His people as:

1. manna (Matthew 4:4; John 6:32-35; 48-51, 58)
2. bread from heaven (John 6:30-35; 48-51, 58)
3. flesh (John 6:51)
4. meat (John 6:27; 55)

> 5. that which causes cessation of both hunger and thirst (John 6:35)
> 6. blood (John 6:53-55).

As shown earlier from John 14 and 15, these are equivalent concepts to:

> 7. abiding in Him (John 15:4)
> 8. dwelling in Him (John 15:17)
> 9. supping (dining) at His table (Revelation 3:20).

It is significant that Jesus taught the principle of receiving daily revelation from Him using the above nine separate illustrations. The number nine is Biblically significant as a number most often associated with the judgment of man and all his works. It marks a completeness, an end, summation, and finality of all of man's accomplishments.[ix]

Overcoming in this specific area of learning to receive and obey revelation from the Lord by dining at His table results not only in everlasting life as noted in the verses above, but also in an invitation to sit with Him in His throne.[16] This very subject is the legacy that Jesus sought to teach and leave for all those who would be sheep (John 10:27) and hear His voice.

Will You Also Go Away?
The Pharisees were not the only ones who were offended by Jesus' reference to the need to receive revelation manna, or meat from Him. The Pharisees were the intellectuals who

---

[16] *Revelation 3:21: To him that overcometh will I grant to sit with me in my throne, even as I also overcame, and am set down with my Father in his throne.*

searched the Scriptures yet did not find eternal life, though they sincerely thought so.[17]

Many people today think they have found the full riches of eternal life because they became born again. Salvation is not the question here, since salvation is clear from Romans 10:9 and 10 upon the confession of Jesus as Lord.

If salvation is all that is available to believers, then this would certainly be sufficiently wonderful! But the rewards of sitting in the Master's throne, of being a part of the kingdom – these are determined by our relationship with the Lord. Is our continuing relationship based upon spending intimate time in His presence now around His table? Or is church our only contact? Our position as priest in a royal priesthood, and as members of a chosen generation (I Peter 2:9) requires more than a passive, spectator relationship with the Lord because the Lord requires all of our heart, not just a portion of it.

Amos 8:11-13
*Behold, the days come, saith the Lord GOD, that **I will send a famine in the land, not a famine of bread, nor a thirst for water, but of hearing the words of the LORD:***
*And they shall wander from sea to sea, and from the north even to the east, **they shall run to and fro to seek the word of the LORD, and shall not find it.***
In that day shall the fair virgins and young men faint for thirst.
They that swear by the sin of Samaria, and say, Thy god, O Dan, liveth; and, The manner of Beersheba liveth; even they shall fall, and never rise up again.

---

[17]*John 5:39: Search the scriptures; for in them ye think ye have eternal life: and they are they which testify of me.*

Notice that the idolatry of verse 13 above is in direct contrast with the revelation words of the Lord of verse 11. Without continual revelation to sustain God's people, the resulting famine of revelation-manna will lead directly to idolatry as heinous as the sin of Samaria.[x] We see it today all around us.

Jesus, through His death and resurrection, provided the means for us to hear His revelation to God's people. He dramatized the message using numerous comparisons to physical food, teaching it to both the Pharisees and disciples. Upon His death and resurrection He restored hearing revelation to all of God's people.

Not All Are Hungry

Sadly, not every believer in Christ is hungry to hear this message. In John chapter 6 for example, many disciples no longer walked with Jesus when he taught it to them.

John 6:60-66
Many therefore of his disciples, when they had heard this, said, This is an hard saying; who can hear it?
*When Jesus knew in himself that his disciples murmured at it, he said unto them, **Doth this offend you?***
What and if ye shall see the Son of man ascend up where he was before?
It is the spirit that quickeneth; the flesh profiteth nothing: the words [rhema] *that I speak unto you, they are spirit, and they are life.*
But there are some of you that believe not. For Jesus knew from the beginning who they were that believed not, and who should betray him.
And he said, Therefore said I unto you, that no man can come unto me, except it were given unto him of my Father.

Would You Like Some More Manna, Son?

From that time many of his disciples went back, and walked no more with him.

Every Christian would do well to ask the question that Jesus asked His disciples, "Does this offend you?" To offend (*skandalizo*) means to vex, offend, excite feelings of repugnance, shock, or cause to stumble. The same question is still pertinent today. Our flesh will always resist the message of this book. The message is still offensive to some people today.

The words that Jesus spoke then were inspired utterance, *rhema*. The revelation words He speaks today into your spirit are also *rhema*. Some Christians are offended that others hear such words from the Lord today. This is the very subject that separated the men from the boys **among even the disciples** in Jesus' day. It is still doing that now.

Are you offended by the need to hear His voice or are you blessed and eager to seek His face and hear what He has to say specifically to you? Are you blessed that other brothers and sisters are learning to spend time in His presence and be sheep that hear His voice, or does the concept irk you like it did the Pharisees?

There are many born again Christians today who will walk away from the very concept of hearing daily revelation from their Lord and Savior. But *rhema* words from Him are spirit and they are life. They are not optional to the Christian walk.

John 6:67-69
*Then said Jesus unto the twelve, **Will ye also go away?***
*Then Simon Peter answered him, Lord, **to whom shall we go?** thou hast the words* [rhema] *of eternal life.*

And we believe and are sure that thou art that Christ, the Son of the living God.

Remember: Let our response be as Peter, "Lord, to whom shall we go? You have the words (revelation, *rhema*) of eternal life."

May our prayer be, "Lord, we are sure that you are the One who is that Anointed One, the Son of the Living God, who lovingly gives revelation manna with which to live each day. Lord Jesus, may we be faithful to utilize this trust, for which you gave your life, and for which the Holy Spirit continues to draw your people near who have ears to hear."

Jesus is still knocking. Are you willing to submit to the Holy Spirit and learn from Him how to open the door?

Chapter 6

Eating the Bread of Life: How to Minister to the Lord

My heart has always responded with joy to the words of the famous hymn "In the Garden":

I come to the garden alone,
While the dew is still on the roses;
And the voice I hear, falling on my ear,
The Son of God discloses.

He speaks, and the sound of His voice,
Is so sweet the birds hush their singing;
And the melody that He gave to me
Within my heart is ringing.

I'd stay in the garden with Him
Tho the night around me be falling;
But He bids me go- through the voice of woe,
His voice to me is calling.

Chorus
And He walks with me,
and He talks with me,
And He tells me I am His own;
And the joy we share
as we tarry there
None other has ever known.[xi]

81

No one can take another person to the spiritual garden, "my secret place" as Dwight Moody called it. But once there, the Holy Spirit will guide them into the Lord's presence. Jesus wanted to go to the *physical* garden, even knowing what lay ahead, so we could ever more come to the *spiritual* garden with Him. Once one hears the voice of the Lord in the garden of his heart, it becomes the most desirable place to stay, a refreshing to the soul, and a strengthening for the work ahead. It is in this context that the promise of Jeremiah 33:3, and the example of Moses, Aaron, and Samuel draws us to a deeper hunger to hear from Him.

Jeremiah 33:3
Call unto me, and I will answer thee, *and shew thee great and mighty things, which thou knowest not.*

Psalms 99:5-9
Exalt ye the LORD our God, and worship at his footstool; for he is holy.
Moses and Aaron among his priests, and Samuel among them that call upon his name; they called upon the LORD, and he answered them.
He spake unto them in the cloudy pillar: they kept his testimonies, and the ordinance that he gave them.
Thou answeredst them, O LORD our God: *thou wast a God that forgavest them, though thou tookest vengeance of their inventions.*
Exalt the LORD our God, and worship at his holy hill; for the LORD our God is holy.

King David knew about spending time with the Lord. While I like to call it "Dining at His table" from Revelation 3:20, David referred to it as "dwelling in the secret place of the most High," as the temple, the tabernacle and as His house.

Psalms 91:1, 9
He that dwelleth in the secret place of the most High *shall abide under the shadow of the Almighty.*

Because thou hast made the LORD, *which is my refuge, even the most High,* **thy habitation;**

Psalms 27:4-5
One thing have I desired of the LORD, that will I seek after; that I may **dwell in the house of the LORD** *all the days of my life, to behold the beauty of the LORD, and* **to inquire in his temple.**
For in the time of trouble he shall hide me in his pavilion: **in the secret of his tabernacle** *shall he hide me; he shall set me up upon a rock.*

David was not talking about living in the temple with the Levites. He was talking about living in the spirit realm in the throne room. He was talking about living in the secret place of the most High, dining at His table, eating His manna, rejoicing in His presence. It was what Moses referred to as the meeting place at the tabernacle. All these are descriptions for a personal, intimate relationship with the Lord. In fact it was the potential loss of this relationship that humbled David at the prophet Nathan's pronouncement of David's sin with Bathsheba when he said "You [David] are the man."

In Psalm 51 David cried out a response to God, pleading with Him not to take His Spirit from him. Why? So that he would not lose the joy of His presence when he went to visit with the Lord at His table in his secret place.

Psalms 51:10-11
Create in me a clean heart, O God; and renew a right spirit
within me.
Cast me not away from thy presence*; and take not thy holy*
spirit from me.

Can we not ask the Lord to reveal Himself to us? Can we not
ask Him to show us great and mighty things that we do not
know, too? Won't He help us find Him in the secret place, in
His sanctuary? Will He not answer those who ask for
understanding of His written Word? Would He give His
children anything less than His Holy Spirit?[18] Will not the Holy
Spirit guide you into all truth through speaking that which He
hears to you[19] and showing you things to come? What a
wonderful reason to stay in the garden with Him, dining at His
table.

---

[18]*Luke 11:11-13: If a son shall ask bread of any of you that is a father, will*
he give him a stone? or if he ask a fish, will he for a fish give him a serpent?
Or if he shall ask an egg, will he offer him a scorpion?
If ye then, being evil, know how to give good gifts unto your children: how
much more shall your heavenly Father give the Holy Spirit to them that ask
him?

[19]*John 14:26: But the Comforter, which is the Holy Ghost, whom the Father*
will send in my name, he shall teach you all things, and bring all things to
your remembrance, whatsoever I have said unto you.

John 16:7-8: Nevertheless I tell you the truth; It is expedient for you that I
go away: for if I go not away, the Comforter will not come unto you; but if I
depart, I will send him unto you.
And when he is come, he will reprove the world of sin, and of righteousness,

John 16:13: Howbeit when he, the Spirit of truth, is come, he will guide you
into all truth: for he shall not speak of himself; but whatsoever he shall hear,
that shall he speak: and he will shew you things to come.

Matthew 11:28-30
Come unto me, all ye that labour and are heavy laden, and I will give you rest.
Take my yoke upon you, and learn of me; for I am meek and lowly in heart: and ye shall find rest unto your souls.
For my yoke is easy, and my burden is light.

The "burden" of coming to Jesus in the garden of your heart is easy indeed. Keeping daily appointments with Him is part of taking His yoke upon you, for the yoke is more a yoke of partnership with the Master than a yoke of labor. Notice that spiritual rest as a result of coming into the presence of the Lord, *precedes* taking up His yoke, not the other way around.

Let Jesus Teach You
Jesus is the Master Teacher. Just as He taught His disciples, so will He teach you when you come to Him for lessons. We learn of Him both from the written Word, and as noted previously, we learn of Him from His spoken *rhema*. This was a lesson the Apostle Paul went to Arabia to learn.

Galatians 1:15-2:2
But when it pleased God, who separated me from my mother's womb, and called me by his grace,
*To reveal his Son in me, that I might preach him among the heathen; **immediately I conferred not with flesh and blood:***
Neither went I up to Jerusalem to them which were apostles before me; but I went into Arabia, and returned again unto Damascus.
***Then after three years I went up to Jerusalem** to see Peter, and abode with him fifteen days.*
But other of the apostles saw I none, save James the Lord's brother.

Now the things which I write unto you, behold, before God, I lie not.

Afterwards I came into the regions of Syria and Cilicia;

And was unknown by face unto the churches of Judaea which were in Christ:

But they had heard only, That he which persecuted us in times past now preacheth the faith which once he destroyed.

And they glorified God in me.

Then fourteen years after I went up again to Jerusalem *with Barnabas, and took Titus with me also.*

And I went up by revelation, *and communicated unto them that gospel which I preach among the Gentiles, but privately to them which were of reputation, lest by any means I should run, or had run, in vain.*

Paul was perhaps the most Scripturally literate believer of the first Century. He didn't go to Arabia to hide out and let the dust settle from killing Christians, and he didn't go there to learn the Bible better. He went to learn how to interact with Jesus through the Holy Spirit. He went to learn how to be led by the Spirit.

As brazen as he was before his conversion on the road to Damascus, Paul was even more focused and fearless afterward. He went to Arabia because he was led by the Spirit to do so. There he learned to hear, and submit to, the risen Lord. During this time Paul learned to walk by revelation just as Ananias had learned to walk in Acts 9:10-18.

Jesus had to learn to walk by revelation, too.

Luke 3:21-22

Now when all the people were baptized, it came to pass, that Jesus also being baptized, and praying, the heaven was opened,

And the Holy Ghost descended in a bodily shape like a dove upon him, and a voice came from heaven, which said, Thou art my beloved Son; in thee I am well pleased.

Luke 4:1-2, 14
And Jesus being full of the Holy Ghost returned from Jordan, **and was led by the Spirit into the wilderness,**
Being forty days tempted of the devil. And in those days he did eat nothing: and when they were ended, he afterward hungered.

And Jesus returned in the power of the Spirit *into Galilee: and there went out a fame of him through all the region round about.*

After being baptized by John in the Jordan River, Jesus received the Holy Spirit (Luke 3:21-22). In the ensuing forty days in the wilderness, Jesus learned to walk in the Spirit. Learning to walk in the Spirit is a process, and it doesn't come automatically. Neither does it necessarily come overnight. But as a person faithfully seeks the *face* of the Lord rather than His *hand*, the Lord faithfully responds by speaking words into their spirit through the Holy Spirit.

Learning to trust His words to you takes time to develop. So don't be discouraged or anxious. Be still, and cultivate that quiet, inner stillness before Him. You are seeking to enter His presence to be with your first love. One doesn't have to talk to be blessed being in the presence of the one they love with all their heart.

Notice that Jesus was led by the Spirit into the wilderness, but returned from the wilderness in power. Being led by the Spirit involves heeding the Master's voice, a flowing of *rhema* from Holy Spirit within[20].

God's Desire is to Talk With All of His People

In the Old Testament, God left the job of receiving and communicating His revelation to the prophets. However, God's true heart was for all the people to be able to receive revelation from Him as a kingdom of priests.

Exodus 19:5, 6, 9

*Now therefore, **if ye will obey my voice indeed**, and keep my covenant, **then ye shall be a peculiar treasure** unto me above all people: for all the earth is mine:*

And ye shall be unto me a kingdom of priests, and an holy nation. These are the words which thou shalt speak unto the children of Israel.

*And the LORD said unto Moses, **Lo, I come unto thee in a thick cloud, that the people may hear when I speak with thee**, and believe thee for ever. And Moses told the words of the people unto the LORD.*

Some holy thunder and lightning, a thick cloud, a loud trumpet voice, fire and an earthquake intimidated the people. They thought twice about sharing Moses' privilege of hearing the Lord's voice. They thought they were going to die if God spoke to them, and asked Moses to relay any messages.[21] In so doing,

---

[20] *John 7:38-39*
He that believeth on me, as the scripture hath said, out of his belly shall flow [reo, a form of *rhema*] *rivers of living water. (But this spake he of the Spirit, which they that believe on him should receive: for the Holy Ghost was not yet given; because that Jesus was not yet glorified.)*

[21] *Exodus 20:19 - And they said unto Moses, Speak thou with us, and we will hear: but let not God speak with us, lest we die.*

they abdicated from a tremendous privilege – to commune with the Lord directly and hear His voice.

Later God showed Himself to the 70 elders of Israel, Moses, and three others (Exodus 24:9-11). Still later God told Moses that He would meet him at the mercy seat of the ark (Exodus 25:22) in the most holy place of the tabernacle (Exodus 26:33). God wanted to talk to all the people, but their fear prevented it. Fear, usually in the form of anxiety, still stops some people today even though Jesus tore the veil of separation into the most holy place.[22] The Lord clearly wants us to commune with Him with no more veils of separation.

Samuel Learned to Minister to the Lord

With the establishment of the priestly order of access into the most holy part of the temple, God limited Himself to conversing with the designated priest one time a year,[23] and regularly to the prophets.

The record of Samuel as a young boy in the temple reflects a time when there was little revelation being given because the priestly office was being neglected.

1 Samuel 3:1
And the child Samuel ministered unto the LORD before Eli. ***And the word of the LORD was precious in those days; there was no open vision.***

---

[22] *Luke 23:45 - And the sun was darkened, and the veil of the temple was rent in the midst.*

[23] Hebrews 9:1-14; Exodus 25:21-22; 30:10

The word of the Lord in this verse refers to revelation. The reason it was precious, i.e. rare, in those days is because there was little effective ministering to the Lord being done by the priest. Hence there was no open vision. To prevent the loss of the lamp of God's presence and the light of His revelation, the Lord began raising up Samuel by first teaching Him to hear His voice.

1 Samuel 3:3-7
And ere the lamp of God went out in the temple of the LORD, where the ark of God was, and Samuel was laid down to sleep;
That the LORD called Samuel*: and he answered, Here am I.*
And he ran unto Eli, and said, Here am I; for thou calledst me. And he said, I called not; lie down again. And he went and lay down.
And the LORD called yet again*, Samuel. And Samuel arose and went to Eli, and said, Here am I; for thou didst call me. And he answered, I called not, my son; lie down again.*
Now Samuel did not yet know the LORD, neither was the word of the LORD yet revealed unto him.

Samuel, dedicated from birth for service to the Lord, learned to hear God's voice during the night. Old sleeping Eli, the priest, didn't hear it. His spiritual ears should have been attuned, but he had long since failed to execute his office responsibly[24]. Samuel's heart was to minister to the Lord. Samuel, not Eli, heard His voice. But even in the midst of spiritual slumber, Eli recognized the signature of the way of the Lord – revelation words – *rhema* to His people.

In verse seven, a fantastic truth emerges. Samuel did not know how to hear the voice of the Lord because he did not yet know

---

[24] I Samuel 2:12-17

the Lord. Samuel didn't have an active relationship with Him yet.

Samuel had his one-way service duties in the temple down pat. He was dedicated from birth to serve in the temple, and he was dutifully obeying Eli's direction in spite of the pervasive evil generated by Eli's sons. But Samuel did not yet have a two-way relationship with the Lord. A two-way relationship is what hearing the voice of the Lord is all about.

What is it to minister to the Lord? In a nutshell, it is man's part of cultivating an intimate relationship with the Lord. It can occur only after one is born again because only the Holy Spirit can lead a person into the presence of the Lord. The Levitical ministering to the Lord in the tabernacle involved many things in the physical realm – the performance of sacrifices, blessings, burning incense, etc. It involved cleansing from sin. But central to all ministering to the Lord was (and still is today) the heart of worship, and the heart of obedience to do what the Lord says. Ministering to the Lord is done with a heart that simply wants to be in the presence of the Lord, not with an agenda, and not with burdens, but just to be with one's first love.

Worship and obedience to revelation received are two prominent characteristics of those who minister before the Lord. Thanksgiving and praise are two more ingredients for those who would come before the Lord to minister to Him in His sanctuary.

Psalms 100:1-5
Make a joyful noise unto the LORD, all ye lands.
Serve the LORD with gladness: ***come before his presence with singing.***

Know ye that the LORD he is God: it is he that hath made us, and not we ourselves; we are his people, and the sheep of his pasture.
Enter into his gates with thanksgiving, and into his courts with praise: *be thankful unto him, and bless his name.*
For the LORD is good; his mercy is everlasting; and his truth endureth to all generations.

I am convinced that the Lord has an individual curriculum for each believer who desires to spend time with Him to learn. The purpose of the Holy Spirit is to guide each believer into all truth, and draw them into a living relationship with the King, Jesus. Notice how the Lord worked with Samuel.

1 Samuel 3:8-10
And the LORD called Samuel again the third time. *And he arose and went to Eli, and said, Here am I; for thou didst call me. And Eli perceived that the LORD had called the child.*
Therefore Eli said unto Samuel, Go, lie down: and it shall be, if he call thee, that thou shalt say, Speak, LORD; for thy servant heareth. So Samuel went and lay down in his place.
And the LORD came, and stood, and called as at other times, *Samuel, Samuel. Then Samuel answered, Speak; for thy servant heareth.*

In answering, Samuel showed the childlike trust that Jesus prized in Matthew 18:1-4 in response to the disciples' question, "Who is the greatest in the kingdom of heaven?"

Matthew 18:1-4
At the same time came the disciples unto Jesus, saying, Who is the greatest in the kingdom of heaven?)
And Jesus called a little child unto him, and set him in the midst of them,

*And said, Verily I say unto you, **Except ye be converted, and become as little children, ye shall not enter into the kingdom of heaven.***
Whosoever therefore shall humble himself as this little child, the same is greatest in the kingdom of heaven.

As young Samuel was humble, ministering before the Lord, so must we be humble if we would enter the kingdom of heaven. We dare not become so sophisticated in our theology that we refuse to seek and hear the voice of the Lord as a little child, and respond as willingly with a pure heart like Samuel. We dare not respond with disbelief to things of the Holy Spirit, pushing Him away when He tries to draw us closer to the lips of the Lord.

Though we don't want to grieve the Spirit, we clearly do so every time we remain as deaf and insensitive to His leading as Eli. We dare not be as the Pharisees, who found their own doctrinal reasons to "Scripturally" judge both the message and the Messenger wrongly.   There are those who will read this book and find "doctrinal" reasons to push aside the message. But at the judgment seat of Christ, some may have to answer why they did not pursue a closer relationship with the Master on His terms instead of their own.

Our relationship with the Lord must be at least close enough to learn how to receive revelation manna from Him often enough to sustain ourselves and our ministries, and know the joy of His presence. We should want to be invited to sit with Him in His throne (Revelation 3:21) by being faithful to overcome every doubt, every inhibition, every doctrinal wall, every hint of spiritual laziness, and lack of spiritual hunger to seek His face daily.

Is not this the message of the treasure in the field, and the pearl of great price in Matthew 13:44-46? Should we not take stock of what we are doing, and choose now to spend time with Him at His table each day?

Matthew 13:44-46
Again, the kingdom of heaven is like unto treasure hid in a field; the which when a man hath found, he hideth, and for joy thereof goeth and selleth all that he hath, and buyeth that field.
Again, the kingdom of heaven is like unto a merchant man, seeking goodly pearls:
Who, when he had found one pearl of great price, went and sold all that he had, and bought it.

May we be as Samuel, not as Eli before the Lord.

Jesus, the Revelation Giver
Jesus came to give us light. What light did He give? Most Christians agree that the light He gave was revelation. But did His revelation stop with the words written in red in the gospels of Matthew, Mark, Luke and John? Of course not. Just as He gave revelation to Ananias in Acts 9, and to John in the book of Revelation, He continues to give revelation today to His church.

Luke 2:25-32
*And, behold, there was a man in Jerusalem, whose name was Simeon; and the same man was just and devout, waiting for the consolation of Israel: **and the Holy Ghost was upon him.***
***And it was revealed unto him by the Holy Ghost,** that he should not see death, before he had seen the Lord's Christ.*
***And he came by the Spirit** into the temple: and when the parents brought in the child Jesus, to do for him after the custom of the law,*

Then took he him up in his arms, and blessed God, and said,
Lord, now lettest thou thy servant depart in peace, according to
thy word:
For mine eyes have seen thy salvation,
Which thou hast prepared before the face of all people;
*A **light** to **lighten** the **Gentiles**, and the glory of thy people*
Israel.

Simeon was led by the Holy Spirit to prophesy over the Christ
child. He proclaimed that Jesus would be a light to lighten, or
give revelation, to the Gentiles. John is said to have written the
book of revelation around 95 AD. Regardless of the exact year
written, it is certainly clear that Jesus gave John the revelation
several decades *after* the crucifixion. Obviously, Jesus *still*
gives light to lighten the Gentiles.

Interestingly, I've run into believers who adamantly feel that to
write down revelation that the Lord gives an individual today is
tantamount to adding to the Scriptures in violation of the
warning of Revelation 22:18. But the careful reader will note
that the warning of verse 18 pertains to John's book alone, and
the Lord was also careful to issue definitive instructions for the
use and dissemination of this revelation in chapter one. The
Lord will often tell the recipient what to do with the revelation
manna He dispenses. No one today who has ever received
revelation from the Lord would ever be foolish enough to add it
to the canonized Bible as Scripture.

Cannot the Lord take us up into heaven as He did to the Apostle
Paul if He chooses? There are many deep things He wants to
reveal to us and our church as the Bride of Christ is being
readied by the Holy Spirit in these end times. Can't we take
notes in school? Why not take notes in the school that Jesus
and the Holy Spirit run for those who humble themselves as

children before Him? Do these notes classify as Scripture? No, no more than would spoken prophecy.

The message of the book of Revelation completes the Scripture just as the Lord intended. Prophecy today, whether written or spoken, is always a message to edify, exhort, and comfort the people present (I Corinthians 14:3), and the speaking by revelation, word of knowledge, prophesying, or by doctrine of I Corinthians 14:6 is also for an audience of the people present for that message.

Inspired words are inspired words, whether written or spoken, and they come from the Father, from the Lord Jesus Christ, or from the Holy Spirit[xii] as guidance, teaching, and direction. To label this process as a violation of Revelation 22:18 reflects a misunderstanding of the purpose of communication from the Lord today for His church.

How Jesus Received Revelation on Earth
Jesus received revelation in several different ways. For example, upon completion of His baptism as well as on the Mount of Transfiguration, an audible voice was heard as revelation from above. Audible revelation happened to Paul on the road to Damascus when the Lord witnessed to him (Acts 9:1-7). The more common "verbal" revelation, however, is received as an inner voice. Consider how Jesus described this process in John 3.

John 3:31-34
He that cometh from above is above all: he that is of the earth is earthly, and speaketh of the earth: he that cometh from heaven is above all.
And what he hath seen and heard, *that he testifieth; and no man receiveth his testimony.*

He that hath received his testimony hath set to his seal that God is true.
For he whom God hath sent speaketh the words [rhema] *of God: for God giveth not the Spirit by measure unto him.*

Once again we see that *rhema* words are revelation words received from above, in this case from God. Without the Spirit, there could be no inner receipt of spiritual communication from above. As noted previously, the Spirit flows (*reo*, a root form of *rhema*) out of the belly (John 7:38), and is likened to rivers (yes RIVERS!) of living water. These rivers of revelation provide the ammunition for many of the works noted in the book of Acts, all of the miracles of faith in Hebrews chapter 11, the faith-building process of Romans 10:17, and the building of the Lord's church of Matthew 16:17-19. But there is more.

John 5:30
*I can of mine own self do nothing: as I hear, I judge: and my judgment is just; **because I seek not mine own will**, but the will of the Father which hath sent me.*

We learned in John 3:34 that Jesus received *rhema* revelation from the Father by the Holy Spirit. Here in John 5:30, it is apparent that Jesus could do nothing of His own will, but everything of the Father's will through both hearing and performing revelation from the Father. Where did Jesus go to hear these words of revelation? He often received them in a solitary place – a place alone where He could quietly pray.[25] For example, he stayed up all night to pray for the revelation to choose His twelve apostles from among many disciples (Luke 6:12-13).

---

[25] Matthew 6:6; Luke 5:16; Mark 1:35, 6:46

This is how we are to function today also as imitators of Christ – first hearing *rhema,* i.e. revelation manna from around His dining table, and then carefully performing it. Without Him we can do nothing (John 15: 5). Why? Because He provides the revelation we need to function for Him, to carry out His orders as He builds His church. Without revelation from Him we can do nothing.[26]

John 14:10-12
*Believest thou not that I am in the Father, and the Father in me? **the words** [rhema] **that I speak unto you I speak not of myself: but the Father that dwelleth in me, he doeth the works.***
Believe me that I am in the Father, and the Father in me: or else believe me for the very works' sake.
Verily, verily, I say unto you, He that believeth on me, the works that I do shall he do also; and greater works than these shall he do; because I go unto my Father.

The truths of John 3:34 and 5:30 are again reiterated in John 14:10 – that Jesus received and spoke the revelation *rhema* words which came from the Father, and by speaking them Jesus was able to do the works that astonished and testified to the world. Can you see the awesome impact for believers who are willing to apply themselves to receiving revelation manna from the Lord today? This is precisely the implication and means by which the believer *today* can perform the works of Jesus Christ and even greater.

---

[26] *John 15:5 - I am the vine, ye are the branches: He that abideth in me, and I in him, the same bringeth forth much fruit: for without me ye can do nothing.*

Did Jesus raise people from the dead? You can too according to the performance of revelation you receive. Did He heal the sick, did He preach inspired words, and cast out demons? You can do all of these things as He gives the words of revelation and direction garnered from conversations around His table.

Whether you like to use the term dining table, sanctuary, garden, presence, throne room, tabernacle, mercy seat, secret place, or dwelling place (or any other Biblically descriptive reference I've not listed here), meeting Him for your daily marching orders is crucial to walking as He did. As He is, so are we in this world (I John 4:17) because as He *did* to receive church-building revelation, *so are we to do.* **W**e must open the door, and dine with Him.

Show Me Thy Way

David was a man who knew the value of seeking the Lord's way, which was revealed as he ministered to the Lord through singing psalms. Perhaps more than any other example in the Scripture, David exemplified the heart necessary to walk by the Spirit. Consider that this man, called a man after God's own heart, longed for the day that He could see the Messiah. He looked forward, by revelation, with a certainty that He would one day see the fruit of his loins through his lineage, the Christ (Acts 2:30). This man knew the joy and continual benefits of seeking to be in the Lord's presence daily. He learned how to minister to the Lord by asking the Lord how He wanted to be ministered to.

Psalms 25:4-5
Shew me thy ways, O LORD; teach me thy paths.
Lead me in thy truth, and teach me: for thou art the God of my salvation; on thee do I wait all the day.

Psalms 25:9-14
The meek will he guide in judgment: and the meek will he teach his way.
All the paths of the LORD are mercy and truth unto such as keep his covenant and his testimonies.
For thy name's sake, O LORD, pardon mine iniquity; for it is great.
What man is he that feareth the LORD? him shall he teach in the way that he shall choose.
His soul shall dwell at ease; and his seed shall inherit the earth.
The secret of the LORD is with them that fear him; and he will shew them his covenant.

Remember: The Lord has covenanted with each one of us who have called upon Jesus Christ and asked Him to be our Lord. He has allowed us the privilege of ministering to Him, and to eat revelation manna at His table. Our hunger to know Him correlates to hunger for physical food, something we need every day. Sometimes we may need the Lord's help to become more hungry.

An appetite can be built, and the Lord has the most amazing restaurant that never closes, and whose menu is always changing. The meals grow more satisfying and nourishing each time we sit down to eat. Without revelation food from Him, we can do nothing. Let us be as Samuel – diligent to minister to the Lord each day, and ready to affirm, *"Speak Lord, for Thy servant heareth."* And may we be eager to say, "yes Lord, I will obey quickly."

Chapter 7

Become Confident in His Voice

One of the most fascinating Old Testament records concerning God's will for Israel (and His people still today) is contained in Deuteronomy chapter eight. In the opening verses of this chapter, God declared the purpose of the wilderness wandering. I think of this period as God's boot camp. There are terrific lessons in this record for believers today.

Deuteronomy 8:1-2
All the commandments which I command thee this day shall ye observe to do, that ye may live, and multiply, and go in and possess the land which the LORD sware unto your fathers.
*And thou shalt remember all the way which the LORD thy God led thee these forty years in the wilderness, **to humble thee, and to prove thee, to know what was in thine heart, whether thou wouldest keep his commandments, or no.***

God never intended for Israel to be inferior to the unbelieving occupants of the Promised Land. Though they could have walked to the Promised Land in eleven days, God knew they were still carrying cursed baggage from Egypt. For example, they complained continually despite the amazing demonstration of God's constant care in crossing the Red Sea. They complained almost immediately after gaining freedom from the pharaoh, and they complained three short days after God's supernatural destruction of pharaoh's impressive army.

What would make Israel superior to the Caananites was a superior God. What would make Israel learn to work alongside that superior God was obedience and reliance – hence the wilderness boot camp. God's people needed to learn how to depend on God. This required learning humility. God used the wilderness as a practical laboratory to test out their humility in relatively harmless conditions.

Does this sound capricious, or perhaps unnecessary on God's part? Consider what obstacles Israel would subsequently face in the Promised Land. Israel was unskilled in war. Every city had to be taken militarily, and the enemy had weapons, experience, and walls. Israel had nothing except an invincible God. But were the people trained to trust in this Almighty God? Thus the need for the wilderness laboratory.

God would deliver Israel, just like He will deliver His people today, once they learned the art of hearing His voice, and obeying it. Indeed, this is the message of the next verse.

Deuteronomy 8:3
*And he humbled thee, and suffered thee to hunger, and fed thee with manna, which thou knewest not, neither did thy fathers know; **that he might make thee know that man doth not live by bread only, but by every word that proceedeth out of the mouth of the LORD doth man live.***

The one lesson Israel needed to learn in order to be successful in the Promised Land was to hear and obey revelation. How can the Lord be in charge when people refuse to listen to His orders? How can He direct His army when people won't obey the voice of their captain? How will He bring victory to the church today without each member becoming proficient at hearing His voice, and learning to act upon it?

When Moses commanded the people, it was by revelation. The Bible had not been written yet. The commandments of Deuteronomy 8:1 came as revelation to Moses for the people. In verse three, the Lord elaborated that **the entire reason for the wilderness exercise was to learn this one truth: that man is to live by daily revelation from the Lord!**

The reader will surely recognize this verse as the one Jesus quoted to the devil in Matthew 4:4, *But he answered and said, It is written, Man shall not live by bread alone, but by every word* [rhema] *that proceedeth out of the mouth of God.*

Man was to learn how to live by daily *rhema* revelation. If people today want to conquer their Promised Land, they must do it by the revelation manna supplied by God. This is basic training for the church today. It is training for spiritual warfare.

Pride and Revelation Don't Mix
The reason Israel would not hear the Lord's voice was pride. They wanted to argue with God, and they had rebellious hearts. Pride always contradicts God, and thwarts the reception of His revelation.

Hebrews 3:7-19
Wherefore (as the Holy Ghost saith, To day if ye will hear his voice,
Harden not your hearts, as in the provocation, in the day of temptation in the wilderness:
When your fathers tempted me, proved me, and saw my works forty years.
*Wherefore I was grieved with that generation, and said, They do alway err in their heart; **and they have not known my ways.***
So I sware in my wrath, They shall not enter into my rest.)

Take heed, brethren, lest there be in any of you an evil heart of unbelief, in departing from the living God.
But exhort one another daily, while it is called To day; lest any of you be hardened through the deceitfulness of sin.
For we are made partakers of Christ, if we hold the beginning of our confidence stedfast unto the end;
While it is said, To day if ye will hear his voice, harden not your hearts, as in the provocation.
For some, when they had heard, did provoke: howbeit not all that came out of Egypt by Moses.
But with whom was he grieved forty years? was it not with them that had sinned, whose carcases fell in the wilderness?
And to whom sware he that they should not enter into his rest, but to them that believed not?
So we see that they could not enter in because of unbelief.

If Israel had rejected their prideful hardness of heart and learned to hear the Lord's voice, they would not have died in the wilderness. This message is as vital today for God's people as it was for Israel. We will not enter into God's rest if we will not soften our hearts with humility and hear His voice. There is great rest associated with being in the presence of the Lord, hearing His voice.

The Surrendered Heart
A person who hears is one who surrenders to the Holy Spirit. We can ask the Holy Spirit to teach us how to enter the Lord's presence, and learn to hear His voice. This may not happen overnight. The Lord used testing – I didn't say He initiated evil, sickness, disease, torment and other such things that come from satan – but He does test our determination as part of His personalized curriculum to see if we will be faithful to rely on Him or not.

He is the Lord and He does not change (Malachi 3:6). His method is still the same today. If we are faithful in the least, such as in disciplining ourselves to hear His voice, He will lead us from our wilderness boot camp into the Promised Land that He has marked out for us. And make no mistake. Each one of us has a job to do in the body of Christ, a Promised Land to take for His glory. We will find out about our assignment as we learn to dine at His table.

Becoming Humble As A Child
What would have happened if Israel had come to God with the thankful joy of a little child? How blessed the Lord is when we simply desire to spend time with Him! We should be as children in His presence. A parent is loving and encouraging to his or her child, and continually seeks to help steer that child toward wisdom, right thinking, and loving obedience. A child doesn't doubt his parent's love and good intentions for him. Yet Israel both doubted and complained. God became grieved for forty years. It is much more fun to be as a child before the Father and enjoy His presence than it is to complain.

We sometimes complain in subtle ways without knowing it. For example, how many times have we heard Christians ask what the Lord's will is for their lives? "Lord, if it be your will..." is a familiar preface to many prayers. It sounds humble, but it is really a prayer of frustration.

Few children would ever ask what is the will of their parents. Why? Because children are in such close communication with their parents that there is rarely much guessing needed. Questioning the will of the Lord in prayer often arises from a lack of intimacy with Him. Worse, sometimes such questions can stem from a prideful religious spirit wanting to sound humble.

Loving parents constantly provide advice and counsel to their children, especially if they have a hunger to seek it. God freely tells His children what He wants them to do when He wants them to do it. Patiently learning to hear the voice of the Lord is still boot camp, not advanced military training.

Deciding to Grow Up

At this point, many Christians become frustrated. God's requirement is humility before Him. Let me suggest this test as a barometer for our readiness to graduate from boot camp. Do we still complain instead of praise the Lord when things seem to be going awry? Do we make time for coming before Him each day, entering His gates with thanksgiving and His courts with praise? Is fellowship with the Lord or our secular job the higher priority?

Let me also clearly say this: the Lord recognizes the time commitments and requirements of your life. Like the widow's mite in tithing, the Lord knows the sacrifice it takes to place Him first, and recognizes the heart behind your desire to spend time with Him despite the necessity of work, family, and responsibility. If your heart is as the widow's to give your all, small though it may seem, His heart will be to reward you as much as the one who may have hours to seek Him (and who perhaps squanders it).

We must also realize that as we get used to dining at the Lord's table, and He gives us more to do, sometimes we have to "eat on the run." Doing so is much easier if the habits of learning to dine at His table are well established beforehand.

Our flesh **strongly** resists becoming disciplined in this area of spending time alone with the Lord. Perhaps we even become secretly envious of others who have learned the joy of entering

His presence. Some believers flinch when another brother or sister excitedly shares what the Lord told them. Why? Because their flesh makes them feel somehow inadequate compared to the believer who heard from the Lord. A child-like heart won't feel this way at all. A child before the Lord will be as excited as the believer who heard, knowing in himself the joy of hearing the Master's voice. Hearing from the Lord should be as common-place as hearing from our parents.

Heave-ho to Pride
The problem is not insensitivity to other Christians. The problem is the problem of Israel – pride. Pride closes our ears to God. Pride caused Joseph's brothers to become offended by the revelation God gave him regarding his future leadership position, his coat of many colors, and his closeness to their father. Perhaps Joseph was unwise in sharing his dreams to his brothers, but considering the events which followed, Joseph's speaking about his revelation probably made little difference. Nevertheless, wisdom is needed in sharing what the Lord has revealed.

Pride is not easy to lay down. Some of our pride is visible to us, and some is not. But in either case, we must get rid of it – all of it as the Holy Spirit directs - to hear the Lord clearly. Our flesh will fight against the discipline of spending time before the Lord, and learning to be still before Him each day.

Some of us may have spent a lot of time already trying to surrender all to the Lord. In fact sometimes we get prideful about what we have given up to grow in our Christian walk. Some ministers even suppress gift ministries from rising up in their congregations because of pride and control issues. Who me? Prideful? Yes.

I will not soon forget one of the Lord's training programs as He commissioned me to write this book. One day a prophet that I respect and admire called me to tell me a word that the Lord had given to her to help me. I had left both a lucrative secular career and military career to follow the Lord's clear instruction to me. I had taken on a wonderful small country pastorate as well as a growing para-church ministry, and had enjoyed several successful overseas missionary journeys.

Finances had become difficult, and within my heart without realizing it, I had taken on a prideful "suffering for the Lord" attitude. It was subtle, and I didn't recognize it. But God did. Hearing His rebuke, though gently delivered, was nevertheless not a pleasant experience at first. It would have been a whole lot easier to hear the Lord tell me first rather than another minister. But pride blocked my hearing what the Lord probably tried to communicate to me directly. I repented. Another layer of my heart was brought to surrender before the Lord.

I Peter 5:5 tells us that God resists the proud. Humility, being the opposite of pride, was the first lesson the Lord needed to teach Israel in the wilderness in order to help them learn this essential key to receiving consistent revelation - how to hear and obey the voice of the Lord daily.

What joy it was to have my pride revealed, so I could lay it at Jesus' feet! We need to encourage one another to keep on surrendering our heart and our flesh to the Holy Spirit. Neither one can be sufficiently self-laundered to be acceptable in His presence at His table. We must trust the Holy Spirit. We must ask Him to lead us through our wilderness boot-camp, asking Him to help us shed even the pride we didn't know we had.

Our Goal is To Love Him

Are you worried or frustrated about not yet hearing His voice? Don't be. He wants to talk with you more than you want to. He longs to spend heart-to-heart time alone with you. But one key that has helped many believers learn to hear the voice of the Lord is to recognize that our goal is not to hear His voice as much as it is just to spend time with Him in praise and worship. We deeply enjoy ministering to Him by wanting to be with Him. Hearing Him speak into your spirit is a by-product of our relationship with our best friend. He looks forward with joy to being with you for all eternity.

You see, Jesus is in love with us. As much as you long to be in His presence, He is the Beloved in Song of Songs (Song of Solomon) who is waiting for you in the garden.

Song of Solomon 6:2-3
My beloved is gone down into his garden, to the beds of spices, to feed in the gardens, and to gather lilies.
I am my beloved's, and my beloved is mine: he feedeth among the lilies.

Song of Solomon 8:13
Thou that dwellest in the gardens, the companions hearken to thy voice: cause me to hear it.

Make praise your agenda. Make Him your first love and spend time with Him. As you become faithful, He will invite you to His table. There may be some testing, proving the sincerity of your hunger. There may also be obstacles from your flesh trying to compromise and distract your thoughts and your time, pulling them away from intimate time with Him. But stay the course. The Holy Spirit is your friend, commissioned by Jesus to help guide you through this basic training program to help you come closer to Him.

Starting Out

Our youngest son, Mikel was just learning to roll out of bed and praise God first thing each morning. At first he would run through his praise vocabulary within the first five minutes. But he was the one who wanted to commit himself to do this. As he remained faithful to praise the Lord each morning, he began to spend more time with the Lord.

After about a week, the Lord showed him a vision of a huge drinking glass. Then the Lord showed him that just as you wouldn't give a glass with a mere few drops in it to someone requesting a glass of water, so Mikel wasn't to give the Lord just a few drops of praise in the morning. The Lord wanted a full glass!

Praise God for His goodness and grace, and for His readiness to teach us each in ways that we can understand as we grow faithful to spend time with Him. A short while later, my son was led by the Lord to witness further to a nine year old friend that both Mikel and his older brother David had been teaching. Mikel asked the Lord how to do this. The Lord told Him. Mikel obeyed, led the friend to Christ, and later also helped him reach out in faith to begin speaking in tongues!

The Holy Spirit never gives up on us, and we shouldn't become impatient and quit on Him either if we don't see instant results. Let Him help you prune out pride, even the pride you never knew you had. Willingly surrender all the identities about yourself that have been dearer to you than Jesus, the Pearl of great price.

Hebrews Hall of Fame

Great events in the Bible occurred to people who learned to listen to God's still, small voice. *Be still,[27] and know that I am God (Psalms 46:10a)* is an art we must learn with patience and determination. Perhaps the most prominent among believers who learned this lesson are the "hall of fame" forefathers noted in Hebrews.

Hebrews chapter eleven lists a hall of fame of believers who are noted for their great faith. I used to be amazed at their accomplishments out of shear awe of the miracles they helped bring about. But now I realize that, great as the miracles were, faith to perform them is the simple believer's response to prior revelation. Great faith to do miracles comes from great revelation. Great revelation comes from great relationship; a humble and child-like simplicity with the Lord.

Hebrews 11:1-2 (KJV)
Now faith is the substance of things hoped for, the evidence of **things not seen.**
For by it the elders obtained a good report.

Hebrews 11:1-2 (NIV)
Now faith is being sure of what we hope for and certain of **what we do not see.**
This is what the ancients were commended for.

Hebrews 11:1-2 (AMP)
Now faith is the assurance (the confirmation, the title-deed) of the things [we] hope for, being the proof of things [we] do not see and *the conviction of their reality – faith perceiving as real fact* **what is not revealed to the senses.**

---

[27] Lamsa translates this verse from the Aramaic as "Repent, and know that I am God."

For by [faith], *and trust and holy fervor born of faith, the men of old had divine testimony born to them and obtained a good report.*

Faith and Revelation

An important aspect of faith is defined in these verses in Hebrews 11. Faith is exercised when revelation is acted upon. What is meant by the phrases "things not seen", "what we do not see", and "what is not revealed to the senses" in each of the above translations of Hebrews 11:1? Revelation. Revelation knowledge is not gained by the senses. It is gained through the Spirit, and faith rests and acts upon revelation knowledge.

Each of the astonishing miracles chronicled in this chapter all came after revelation was first given. When the recipients acted in faith on the revelation *rhema* they first received from the Lord, the miracles specified in that revelation came about. The things hoped for in Hebrews 11:1 are things about which revelation had been given. When God's people stepped out in faith on this revelation, they received a good report. The NIV declares that this is what the ancients, our Old Testament fathers of faith, were commended for.

Faith is being sure of the revelation received. When we become convinced of the certainty of Jesus' words to us in our private prayer closet, we have no trouble stepping out and performing what He asks. This is precisely why the believers in this chapter were commended!

Greater Faith Requires Greater Relationship

Most of us read Hebrews 11 and wish we could have the kind of faith that a Moses, Abraham, and Enoch had. But the fact is, they didn't have any greater faith than you or I. What they did have was a close familiarity with the sound of the voice of the

Lord. They had developed a relationship such that they trusted His voice enough to heed it. Let's take a look.

Hebrews 11:3
*Through faith we understand that **the worlds were framed by the word** [rhema] **of God**, so that things which are seen were not made of things which do appear.*

The worlds were framed by the *rhema* of God, and we accept this fact in faith. God spoke the world into being with words. God is light. He is the light of revelation. When He spoke, it was inspired utterance, *rhema*. His words had power then, and they have it today. Learn to act on them, and you will see their power first-hand.

Getting it Right
In verse four, Abel's sacrifice was accepted. It was more excellent than Cain's. Although it is not recorded that God told Abel how to make a sacrifice, how would Abel (or his parents, Adam and Eve) have known unless God told him? God would have told Cain the same information. Abel is commended for acting upon this revelation, and his action is called "faith." Cain determined not only to ignore the same information, but substituted his own action in its place. When we "sacrifice" like Abel, we are obeying God's voice and we receive His blessing. When we try to live like Cain on our own religious ideas, we become as the cursed children of Israel who grieved God in the wilderness.

Hebrews 11:5
*By faith Enoch was translated that he should not see death; and was not found, because God had translated him: **for before his translation he had this testimony**, that he pleased God.*

Before Enoch was miraculously taken up, God gave him revelation. Enoch accepted the revelation, and maintained faith in it. Enoch had a sufficiently developed confidence in the Lord that he didn't doubt and wonder about the words. He simply accepted the voice of the Lord as one accepts the words of a close friend.

Little Revelation, Little Pleasing God
Without faith, it is impossible to please God. Think about this for a minute - no faith, no pleasing God.

Hebrews 11:6 (KJV)
But without faith it is impossible to please him: *for he that cometh to God must believe that he is, and that **he is a rewarder of them that diligently seek him.***

Hebrews 11:6 (NIV)
And without faith it is impossible to please God, *because anyone who comes to him **must believe that he exists and that he rewards those who earnestly seek him.***

I'll say it again: without faith, it is impossible to please God. Notice that apart from revelation, the faith referred to in this verse is impossible. The faith part is easy when the personal, intimate relationship with the Lord is a daily occurrence! God rewards those who diligently seek Him. How does He reward them? In many ways that are perhaps too numerous to fully comprehend. But included among them are rewards to those who diligently seek Him, who receive and act upon revelation manna. This pleases God.

Having faith in the words of the Lord to you personally is the easy part. Staying diligent about feeding from His table is the part we tend to neglect.

If there is no revelation, there will be no exercise of faith. If there is no revelation, there will therefore be no pleasing Him.

Three Cheers for Noah

Noah never had Scriptures to read while learning to trust the voice of the Lord. God told Noah by voice into His spirit to build the ark in anticipation of a worldwide flood.

Hebrews 11:7
*By faith Noah, **being warned of God of things not seen as yet, moved with fear, prepared an ark** to the saving of his house; by the which he condemned the world, and became heir of the righteousness which is by faith.*

Noah had faith in the still small voice of the Lord - 120 years worth of faith! He found grace in the eyes of God because he learned to hear, cultivate, and practice the art of listening to and obeying the voice of the Lord. This kind of dependence arises from hunger and desire, not by chance.

Three More Cheers for Abraham

Abraham was no novice to hearing revelation either. Put yourself in his shoes, and you can perhaps get a remote feel for the magnitude of his confidence in the Lord's voice to him.

Hebrews 11:8-10
*By faith Abraham, **when he was called to go out into a place which he should after receive for an inheritance, obeyed; and he went out, not knowing whither he went.***
By faith he sojourned in the land of promise, as in a strange country, dwelling in tabernacles with Isaac and Jacob, the heirs with him of the same promise:
For he looked for a city which hath foundations, whose builder and maker is God.

Abraham was given astonishing revelation to leave home, and travel to find a city described in a revelation. It is not belittling the divinely inspired Bible to say that Abraham did not have a relationship with God's book. He had a relationship with the Lord. Does the fact that Abraham was called a friend of God indicate why he got such revelation?

God did not wave His hand over Abraham and choose him to become a close friend. Abraham chose to draw near to God, learn the sound of His voice, and the more time He spent with the Father, the more the Father was able to reveal to him. The more God revealed to him, the more faith Abraham was able to exercise as he carried out God's *rhema* to him. Hence the miracles.

Testing Abraham's Faith

God even tested Abraham's faith. God demands we lay everything we hold dearer than Him to be offered up to Him. God asked Abraham to sacrifice his promised son, Isaac. Isaac was the one thing Abraham held most dear. Abraham's obedience is overwhelming to contemplate. But let's put aside the obedience for a moment and look instead at his talking relationship with God.

We are to have a better talking fellowship with the Father than Abraham had. This is a result of the finished work of Jesus Christ. Look at the trust Abraham had developed in God's voice to him! What a friendship relationship they had! This type of closeness only grows with frequency of contact. Each of the remaining great men and women mentioned in the rest of Hebrews chapter 11 stepped out on faith, performing revelation they had previously received. Each one learned to hear the voice of the Lord, trust it, and obey it. This is what verse one defined as having faith. We can do the same. The Lord wants us to!

Building Faith

The faith part is really the easy part. We naturally develop trust in people that we draw close to at home and in our communities. We develop trust in the Lord by drawing close to Him also. We like to believe that our close friends will always be there to help us, and oppositely us for them. Trust and believing in another person is a result of contact, time, and opening up the hearts. God opens His heart as we spend time listening to Him.

The relationship building part is fully the responsibility of the individual believer, and it takes time and effort. It won't happen by osmosis. But why not pray that the Holy Spirit will perform His function as a Helper to guide you to become committed to spending time on your knees each day before the Lord in praise and worship?

Every one of us can grow into the same kind of relationship with the Lord that Abraham had. We can receive what the Lord wants to give us – a close and personal fellowship with Him. The faith part is easy when we spend time learning to use the telephone.

In the first century after the day of Pentecost, the telephone lines improved. With no more separation between Jew and Gentile, and with the perfect prayer and praise in the spirit available, believers today have more spiritual tools to work with. Simply by speaking much in tongues, believers can offer up praise, thanksgiving, and conduct spiritual warfare in a language perfectly understood by angels and demons (fallen angels) alike. Tongues of praise, of healing, and of warfare are all important for accomplishing the works of Jesus Christ. It is faith to use the tools that the Lord has given us.

Romans 10:17
So then faith cometh by hearing, and hearing by the word [rhema] **of God** [Christos].

Faith is built by feeding on the inspired words of revelation from God. The Greek word translated as "God" in this verse is literally *Christos*. Faith is built by learning how to hear revelation from Jesus Christ! Putting Hebrews 11:6 together with Romans 10:17 reveals that without learning to hear the sound of His revelation voice, it is literally impossible to please God. This is a very sobering truth for Christians who think that their eternal life rests in an intellectual knowledge of the Scriptures. But it is no more sobering than Mark 16.

Mark 16:17-20
And these signs shall follow them that believe; In my name *shall they cast out devils; they shall speak with new tongues;*
They shall take up serpents; and if they drink any deadly thing,
it shall not hurt them; they shall lay hands on the sick, and they
shall recover.
So then after the Lord had spoken unto them, he was received
up into heaven, and sat on the right hand of God.
And they went forth, and preached every where, **the Lord**
working with them, and confirming the word with signs
following. Amen. *xiii*

Working With Him
The Lord works with those whom He can talk to. He works with those whom he can chasten, rebuke, and prune their branches. He fights with "Pharisee Christians" who want to continue offering their own sacrifices of un-directed good

works, and will ultimately declare to them "I never knew you" because they never had a two-way, close relationship with Him.

If your conversations with the Lord are all one-way connections, then may I suggest you ask the Holy Spirit to lead you into improving the telephone service? Praise and worship calls are always accepted.

The purpose of the Scriptures is to get to know the Lord personally, intimately, and confidently. Our Old and New Testament brothers and sisters did not have written Scriptures available for the common man to read. They had to develop a personal relationship with the Lord instead of an intellectual relationship with the words of the parchment.

I have the greatest joy and respect for the written Word of God. We must realize that the purpose of the written Word is to help us grow into an active relationship with Jesus Christ as a living person. He often speaks to us through His written Word. He will also often speak to us directly by voice into our spirit. He never desired to leave us to a relationship with a book, even His own Book. Instead, He chose to give us His Book in order to help us fall in love and stay in love with Him.

The first century church deteriorated when it fell into literary analysis of Paul's traveling letters, just as the religious rulers of Jesus' day destroyed the portrayal of God's heart with legal analysis. Despite the inspired revelation origin of the words Paul wrote, literary analysis of Paul's letters did not help people learn to depend on the Lord as a personal Savior, Friend, and Counselor. Scriptural depth is a wonderful and vital aid to this end, not an end in itself, because our goal is to grow into an active, personal relationship with our King.

Our King is not dead. He is alive and He speaks daily revelation manna to those who are hungry.

The Coach Makes All the Calls

In these end times of the church age, let's be certain we understand the mechanism by which the Lord communicates to His people. The Lord has called us to be a chosen generation, a royal priesthood, a people marked out for His own purposes to show forth His praise (I Peter 2:9). As we fulfill this calling, He is pleased to lead us into an ever deepening relationship with Him.

This relationship is so valuable to Him, that Jesus willingly submitted to continuous physical and mental torture for us for over 36 hours straight, becoming so marred that he was unrecognizable. He did this so you could have a personal relationship, a close friendship with the Father and with Him. We must commit ourselves to building this relationship *His* way – the way of Abel, not the way of Cain.

Remember: Jesus only asks that we spend time with Him alone each day. We must not leave our first love in the dust of our busy lifestyle. We must not starve ourselves on nutrition-less fast food religion, or eat someone else's leftovers. We must not confuse corporate worship and Christian fellowship with others as a replacement for building a personal relationship with the Lord. We need to come home for supper each night, to the elegance of His table, and the intimacy of His heart.

Chapter 8

Becoming Best Friends with the Lord

One of the most thrilling sections of Scripture to me is what Jesus taught His apostles during the walk to the garden. If you knew that tonight would be the last time you could be with your family before going on a long and perilous journey that might keep them from ever seeing you again – what would you say to your beloved wife or husband? What would you leave as a legacy in words to your dear children?

Leaving supper after Judas left to betray Him, Jesus told His closest students about His impending departure. He exhorted them to love one another as a badge of their love for the Father. He told them about the necessity for His departure. He told them that He was leaving in order to bring them a Comforter, a Helper, a Guide who would be with them always. During this time, the Lord also told them they were no longer mere servants, but friends.

John 15:10-15
If ye keep my commandments, ye shall abide in my love; even as I have kept my Father's commandments, and abide in his love.
These things have I spoken unto you, that my joy might remain in you, and that your joy might be full.
This is my commandment, That ye love one another, as I have loved you.

Greater love hath no man than this, that a man lay down his life for his friends.
Ye are my friends, if ye do whatsoever I command you.
Henceforth I call you not servants; for the servant knoweth not what his lord doeth: but I have called you friends; for all things that I have heard of my Father I have made known unto you.

The Lord's relationship with His apostles was very dear and intimate. They lived together, traveled, and ministered together. Jesus filled their hearts with awe and wonder as He taught, healed, and delivered multitudes from their afflictions. They stood with Him in the contentions with the Pharisees, and they helped distribute the multiplied five loaves and two fish to thousands of people. Their relationship with the Lord was one of students to their Master, and servants to His needs. They were in awe of the anointed Christ. Yet here in His last moments together, Jesus re-defined their relationship from servants to friends.

The standard of commitment is total for the kind of friends Jesus meant. Friendships today are far more temporary, far less committed, and far more volatile than the true nature of friendship that Jesus spoke to His apostles.

Our love for Jesus is measured by our obedience to Him. What are we to obey? We are to obey what He tells us. In our continuing relationship with the Lord Jesus Christ, our joy is found in obedience to His voice. Our enduring friendship with the Lord is based on both His love to die for us, and on our dying to self for Him by obeying His commandments to us each day. *Ye are my friends, if ye do whatsoever I command you (John 15:14).* The commanding is a present tense; literally it reads "whatsoever I am commanding you". The Lord is commanding us today. Are we willing to receive His words into our spirit today? Are we willing to be His friend today? Are we willing to first hear His voice, and then obey?

If we are willing to hear His voice, and not harden our hearts as in the days of the wilderness wandering, He is willing to change our relationship with Him from servant to friend. Our gracious Redeemer is willing to change our understanding of His written Word from being a set of mere servants' instructions into a continuing dialogue of the Father's heart (John 15:15). Jesus is the Minister of the sanctuary (Hebrews 8:2) where the richest continuing dialogue takes place.

John 15:15
*Henceforth **I call you not servants***; *for the servant knoweth not what his lord doeth:* **but I have called you friends***; for **all things that I have heard of my Father I have made known unto you.***

Hebrews 8:1-2
Now of the things which we have spoken this is the sum: **We have such an high priest***, who is set on the right hand of the throne of the Majesty in the heavens;*
A minister of the sanctuary*, **and of the true tabernacle***, which the Lord pitched, and not man.*

David and Jonathan Bond Together
The depth of friendship meant by the Lord in John 15 is beautifully illustrated by the relationship of Jonathan and David. Jonathan and David's friendship is a type or a pattern of what our relationship should be with the Lord today.[xiv] The record begins in I Samuel, and it reveals astonishing truths concerning how we can fulfill our invitation to become a friend to Jesus Christ.

1 Samuel 18:1-3
*And it came to pass, when he had made an end of speaking unto Saul, that **the soul of Jonathan was knit with the soul of David, and Jonathan loved him as his own soul.***
And Saul took him that day, and would let him go no more home to his father's house.
Then Jonathan and David made a covenant, because he loved him as his own soul.

Jonathan knit his soul together with David. To knit means to bind up together as with bands, to join or to knot, to be in love or to be in league with another.[xv] This was a bonding that was of God, and there was a commitment to each other that ran deeply into each other's souls. It was not unlike Paul and Timothy's relationship as fellow ministers and committed friends. The depth of Jonathan and David's love for each other was so great that David considered it greater than even the love of a man for a woman.

2 Samuel 1:25-27
How are the mighty fallen in the midst of the battle! O Jonathan, thou wast slain in thine high places.
*I am distressed for thee, my brother Jonathan: very pleasant hast thou been unto me: **thy love to me was wonderful, passing the love of women.***
How are the mighty fallen, and the weapons of war perished!

Jesus' love for you is the greatest love you can ever know. You are the object of His love, the reason why He was willing to go through excruciating torture and death with a joy that is incomprehensible to us. He asks us to be still before Him, to counsel with Him, and hear His voice. He asks us to be His friend, to knit our souls together with Him as Jonathan and

David, and with a depth and to a degree that surpasses even the love of a husband for his wife.

Jesus' Love For Us

I once heard a story about a young boy who was being chased through the back alley's of his city. A gang was after him, and as he raced down an alley to escape, he realized there was no way out. He couldn't turn around. To do so would have meant certain capture and death. He had to press forward. As he did, he spied a lone house nearly obscured by surrounding city buildings. A light shone in the window, and the lad ran with all his might toward it. Leaping up the steps, he pounded on the door, desperately hoping to escape his pursuers. Terrified, he looked over his shoulder as he heard steps running toward him.

The door opened, and an old man wordlessly beckoned the boy inside. The old man locked the door behind him and pointed the boy to an upstairs closet. "You are safe here, son", said the old man. The boy stepped inside the closet, his chest still heaving in fear. A loud pounding on the front door made the boy's heart shudder, as the old man worked his way downstairs to the door.

The house became quiet in all but the terror of the boy's heart. To him, an eternity elapsed until he could hear the slow, steady steps of the old man's ascent up the stairs. "If they find me, they'll kill me," shouted the boy's heart over and over, yet the steady certainty of the old man's steps was somehow reassuring. Finally the old man opened the closet door, and told the boy he was safe, and the pursuers had left.

"What did you say to them?" blurted the boy in disbelief. With eyes filled with love, the old man replied, "I told them they couldn't have you, that you belonged to the King." "But they would never stop chasing me, they wanted my blood!" exclaimed the boy, still shaking with fear. In a soft voice the old man told the boy, "It's all right now, they went away satisfied. I gave them my son in place of you."

The Father gave His only Son for you. The pounding fear of our heart is gone. We belong to the King. And the King has called us to be His friend. Can we not spend time with such a friend? Won't He delight in talking with us in the quiet solitude of our closet, alone with Him?

Come into His presence by asking the Helper that He left for you, the Holy Spirit, to help you learn to enter the presence of the King, the keeper of the Father's sanctuary, and become His friend.

David and Jonathan Covenant Together
Not only were David and Jonathan's souls knit together, they also made a commitment, an agreement together. They made a binding covenant between each other.

1 Samuel 18:3
Then Jonathan and David made a covenant, *because he loved him as his own soul.*

The heart that has become knit together with the Lord is a heart that will make a convenant like David and Jonathan. The Lord has already covenanted with us. A covenant is a legal contract. The one He wrote out to us was written with His own blood.

Hebrews 8:6
*But now hath he obtained a more excellent ministry, by how much also **he is the mediator of a better covenant**, which was established upon better promises.*

Becoming Best Friends with the Lord

Hebrews 9:11-15
But Christ being come an high priest of good things to come, by a greater and more perfect tabernacle, not made with hands, that is to say, not of this building;
Neither by the blood of goats and calves, but by his own blood he entered in once into the holy place, having obtained eternal redemption for us.
For if the blood of bulls and of goats, and the ashes of an heifer sprinkling the unclean, sanctifieth to the purifying of the flesh:
How much more shall the blood of Christ, who through the eternal Spirit offered himself without spot to God, purge your conscience from dead works to serve the living God?
*And for this cause he is the **mediator of the new testament** [covenant] , that by means of death, for the redemption of the transgressions that were under the first testament, they which are called might receive the promise of eternal inheritance.*

1 Corinthians 11:25
*After the same manner also he took the cup, when he had supped, saying, **This cup is the new testament** [covenant] **in my blood: this do ye, as oft as ye drink it, in remembrance of me.***

Jesus is our mediator of a new covenant, a new testament, a new legally binding agreement between close friends. When we asked Him to be our Lord, we received both benefits and responsibilities. We renew this covenant afresh every time we spend time before Him in His presence, around His table.

Jesus has extended the cup of friendship to us, and is not afraid to call us His brothers. Jonathan owed David nothing, yet he gave David everything he owned that had any value as a sign of that covenant. In this case, Jonathan gave David his own armor and apparel.

Dining at the Master's Table

1 Samuel 18:4
And Jonathan stripped himself of the robe that was upon him, and gave it to David, and his garments, even to his sword, and to his bow, and to his girdle.

Jonathan was a king's kid. He had plenty of valuable things he could have given his friend David as a token of their covenant of friendship. It is interesting that Jonathan chose to give David his own clothing, sword, bow, and girdle belt.

Has not the Lord given us the same tokens of His bonded covenant with us? Has He not given us His clothing of righteousness? Is His sword not Himself, the Word in the flesh (John 1:14), quickened alive by His Spirit (Hebrews 4:12), our sword of the Spirit (Ephesians 6:17)? Has He not given us the same bow of authority as the armor He was given by the Father when He received *exousia* authority over the powers of darkness (Colossians 1:13) and over heaven and earth (Matthew 28:18)? Has he not given us the girdle belt of truth (Ephesians 6:14), righteousness and faithfulness (Isaiah 11:5)?

Jonathan gave kingly gifts of righteousness and of war to his friend. Jesus is our King, and he is also a Man of war. As friends entrusted with knowing His ways, and not just His acts, are we not also expected to use our spiritual weapons aggressively against the enemies of the King, and within the friendship context (of obedience to His voice) in which they have been given?

Learning to use the King's armor is a fascinating and necessary part of each believer's curriculum. Jesus can teach each one of us to use His spiritual armor. Why not ask Him how?

Best Friends Communicate

Jonathan and David' souls were knit together. They loved each other as brothers. Jonathan delighted greatly in David (I Samuel 19:1). When Saul revealed his intention to kill David, Jonathan signaled a warning. Jonathan told David to hide while Jonathan verified Saul's intentions.

Saul disavowed his stated evil intent against David, and through Jonathan's secret communication, David returned to Saul's table. Later, an evil spirit provoked Saul for a second time to murder David by hurling a spear at him. David escaped, and ultimately had to flee with the help of his wife, Saul's daughter Michal. Jonathan promised to keep David posted of Saul's smallest intention, and then reaffirmed the covenant between them with the words, *"Whatever you want me to do, I'll do for you" (I Samuel 20:4, NIV).*

Ultimately, Jonathan underscored his commitment to David by saying that even if God's blessing is removed from his father Saul, and even if the Lord cuts off all of David's enemies (including Saul), yet a covenant of kindness was to prevail between David and Jonathan, and the Lord's will was to be done regarding even Jonathan's father. Jonathan loved David as he loved his own soul (I Samuel 20:12-17).

The final communication between Jonathan and David was the revelation that Saul was still intent on killing David. Through the signal of an arrow shot, Jonathan told David to flee for good. They wept together and confirmed their commitment to each other before the Lord (I Samuel 20:18-42).

Why is this important? Best friends communicate all their heart with one another. Their soul's are knit together. So must our soul become knit together with our best friend, Jesus, who longs to share all His heart with us too. Jonathan resisted his family in order to honor the commitment to his friend. Our family is important, but Jesus is our friend, and is covenanted with us by His blood for all eternity. Jesus communicates by revelation manna, *rhema*, and we need His continuing manna daily to grow in our relationship with Him.

How marvelous a friend He is! He communicates the deep things of His heart by His Spirit into our spirit. He is our Master Teacher, and our closest friend. He has given us all that we have, including His robe of righteousness, and weapons for battle in the spirit realm. He is our Lord, our Savior, and our best Friend. What a friend we have in Jesus! What a treasure to hear His voice.

Remember: The early part of this chapter related the story of the old man protecting the terrified boy in the alley. We feel the awesome magnitude of the sacrifice of our Father God in giving us His only begotten Son in our place. He did not consent to go for any other reason than because He loved us, and because the Father asked Him to. In doing so, He made it possible to become friends, not merely servants. Like Jonathan, He also gave us His armor – spiritual armor. He gave us His clothing of righteousness. He covenanted with us by His blood.

There is a wonderful song that declares, "When He was on the cross, I was on His mind." You are always on Jesus' mind. How much He longs for your company, your friendship expressed by spending time with Him at His table in His sanctuary. Won't you take the time to dine with Him today?

SECTION III

The Lord Knows The Way

Chapter 9

Deception vs. Revelation: How to Discern the Difference

First Thessalonians 5:23 tells us that God gave us a spirit, a soul, and a body. Praise God that He did! We have privileges to use each of these for His glory. When we become born again, our spirit becomes a Holy Spirit-energized super spirit with which we can do the works of Jesus Christ and even greater according to John 14:12.

One of the greatest impediments to receiving revelation (as well as giving a word of prophecy) is the soul. The soul houses man's emotions, intellect, and reason. Emotions are tremendous assets in loving the unlovable, persevering when the body gets tired, and sustaining hope when reason suggests otherwise. But when it comes to receiving revelation, emotions frequently undermine hearing the voice of the Lord clearly.

A Christian's spiritual "telephone line" to the Lord translates messages through the same message processing center in the soul (i.e. the brain) that the soul itself uses. Hence revelation from the Lord into your spirit "sounds" like your own thoughts' "tone of voice". Put another way, your soul has only one translation device. The voice from the spirit is decoded through the soul, and therefore "sounds" the same as those thoughts which typically originate in the soul. Therefore, regardless of the source of the message, the "sound of the voice" seems to be the same. Christians often look for a grand voice from outside themselves when grappling with the concept of "the voice of the Lord". But the fact is, He most often speaks into your spirit in a quiet inner voice within you.

Because of this, learning to distinguish the sound of the Lord's voice is extremely difficult when peripheral noise, distractions, and interference are not silenced. The most common interference comes from:

1. soulish emotion
2. deceiving spirits
3. pride
4. idolatry
5. fatigue
6. spiritual complacency (laziness)

Soulish Emotion
Often Christians face problems. But too often a Christian magnifies the problem above God. Sometimes this is merely from soulish over-reaction to the problem. The emotions of the soul desperately want to fix what only faith can provide. Frustration can result, fostering soulish anxiety. Sometimes over-magnifying a problem ahead of God is demonically inspired from a spirit of fear, oppression, panic, an emotional spirit, etc. Finally, sometimes the emotion arises from a deceiving spirit providing false information about the problem and its Biblical solution. It may be additionally accompanied by a spirit of pride. Pride keeps the person stewing on the problem and false solutions rather than peacefully waiting on the Lord.

Obviously, these three reasons for soulish emotions only scratch the surface in identifying their sources. Characterizing demons to fit them into finite descriptions is like oversimplifying human personalities by discrete categories and types – the true number of possible permutations are endless! Nevertheless, the point is to begin to understand some key mechanisms which hinder Christians from hearing the voice of the Lord. One of the biggest hindrances is uncontrolled emotions.

Emotional preoccupation with a problem stymies the ability to separate God's still small voice in one's spirit from his or her own inner turmoil. For the Lord to direct our paths, we must be willing to listen. Many Christians bring their troubles to the Lord, and their overwhelming preoccupation with them drowns out the Lord's direction, advice, teaching, and counsel.

As noted in the introduction to this book, preoccupation with self instead of preoccupation with praise and worship produces soul-inspired results. For example, a self-burdened heart prays the problem, but a praise-burdened heart prays solutions and gets successful results.   Ultimately, a heart dwelling on problems is a heart that is dwelling in self-absorbing pride. The problems are held more tightly than God's ability to solve them.

On the other hand, a heart of praise is a heart of humility. God resists pride. His grace goes to the humble (I Peter 5:5 and 6). The ones who come to Him according to His standard (praise and thanksgiving), not their own standard (focus on self, unthankfulness), are the ones who are given more grace. Please don't misunderstand – God hears the emotional cries of His people! It's just that His voice and loving fellowship are able to penetrate hearts prepared with praise.

One of the greatest keys to controlling emotions when learning to hear the voice of the Lord is to cease praying the problem, and develop the discipline to praise the Lord. Praisers are problem solvers, because the Lord works with praisers, not complainers.

A Christian caught up in emotion while trying to ask the Lord for revelation on what to do often prays like this:

> "Lord, I can't stand this problem anymore. You've got to do something. Why haven't you been listening? I need this problem fixed now!"

Surely we have all been tempted to pray like this! Perhaps we have done so without realizing it, through simply holding such an attitude deep in our hearts. Such thinking can be very subtle. At times we may find ourselves seeking the Lord's hand instead of His face - praying our problem instead of praising His power over the situation.

The difference between the hand and the face is the heart in between. A heart concerned more with the solution to the problem prays for the Lord's hand to intervene first. However, the Christian who seeks His face first will praise and worship until, upon entering the Lord's throne-room presence and being invited by Him to ask, will only then lay the problem at His feet. A prayer offered in the Lord's throne room of praise is a lot more effective than a prayer in a closet of despair.

Moses is an awesome example of a man who learned to receive revelation in the midst of extreme emotional circumstances. Who of us would have the peace of mind to hear the voice of the Lord at the edge of the Red Sea? A praiser certainly would.

When over two and a half million complainers were railing at him to take them back to Egyptian slavery, and the world's greatest fighting force was visibly maneuvering for attack, Moses proclaimed to the people, *"Fear ye not, stand still, and see the salvation of the LORD, which he will shew to you to day: for the Egyptians whom ye have seen to day, ye shall see them again no more for ever." (Exodus 14:13).*

How could Moses have such composure in this crisis? Easy. He had a relationship with the Lord. In an earlier conversation a day or two before, the Lord had already told Moses what He was going to do (see Exodus 14:1-12). Moses therefore was easily able to control His emotions and stay at peace within His soul. *If Christians would only check in with the Lord each day and eat at His table, they would be able to possess their own souls and avoid runaway emotions. The personal knowledge Jesus provides at the table enables Christians to keep from being afraid when calamity strikes.*

Our God has counted every hair upon our heads (Matthew 10:30; Luke 12:7). Psalm 139 declares that He knows our downsitting, our uprising, our thoughts afar off. Knowing all this, He also certainly knows our every catastrophe, our every fear, and our every troubling concern. Can't He also help us cross our Jordans and Red Seas? If He already knows our concerns, then shouldn't we be able to express our praises in the midst of emotionally stressful circumstances? Patience in strife does not mean inactivity. It means crank up the praises to God while awaiting His deliverance!

Luke 21:19
In your patience possess ye your souls.

Emotions are wonderful for the Godly purposes for which they were intended. But uncontrolled by the soul, they can be a hindrance to hearing the Lord's voice. They can also become a simple route to demonic influence or possession.

How about the case of a believer who is abundantly blessed, full of joy, and doesn't have any significant problems that result in soulish emotions which distract him or her from hearing the Lord's voice?

This is precisely the situation Christians often face who have not yet developed confidence in the Lord's voice to them. They want so much to hear the Lord's voice, yet being unsure if they have, they become anxious about it. Out of frustration, they turn to someone else's guidance, hoping for the same experience. All of this builds doubt, not faith. The plain fact is, only the Holy Spirit can lead a person into the Lord's presence, and the Holy Spirit can only do so when we trust Him as our Helper, or Guide, to help us with this task.

Anxiety (instead of trust) over whether the Holy Spirit will guide us to hear the Lord's voice can come from soulish emotion. Budding soulish emotion can begin to exercise dominion over a person's spirit in just the same manner as the person whose preoccupation with his problems blocks out revelation from the One who can solve them.

The best method I know for quelling soulish emotion is a good long dose of loud praise. Shout out praises to the Lord for as long as it takes to quiet your soulish emotions within. Ask the Holy Spirit to help you to praise and to lead you. This may take hours for some, and only minutes for others. Isaiah 61:3 speaks of the garment of praise opposing the spirit of heaviness. I can't help but continually refer to one of the most wonderful door openers into the Lord's throne room: the pearls contained in Psalm 100.

Psalms 100:1-5
Make a joyful noise unto the LORD, *all ye lands.*
Serve the LORD with gladness: **come before his presence with singing.**
Know ye that the LORD he is God: it is he that hath made us, and not we ourselves; we are his people, and the sheep of his pasture.
Enter into his gates with thanksgiving, and into his courts with praise: be thankful unto him, and bless his name.
For the LORD is good; his mercy is everlasting; and his truth endureth to all generations.

By far one of the surest methods of stilling emotional distractions is to speak in tongues. Speaking in tongues is perfect praise and it gives a wonderful rest to the soul.[28] This rest helps open the door to enter the Lord's sanctuary, to sit down at His table.

A heart full of continuous praise is a heart that is in control of soulish emotion. Come into the Lord's presence because you want to be with the Lord, not because you have a private agenda, no matter how spiritual that agenda might seem to be.

Isaiah 64:1-5
Oh that thou wouldest rend the heavens, that thou wouldest come down, that the mountains might flow down at thy presence,

---

[28] *Isaiah 28:11-12*
For with stammering lips and another tongue will he speak to this people.
To whom he said, This is the rest wherewith ye may cause the weary to rest; and this is the refreshing: yet they would not hear.

As when the melting fire burneth, the fire causeth the waters to boil, to make thy name known to thine adversaries, that the nations may tremble at thy presence!
When thou didst terrible things which we looked not for, thou camest down, the mountains flowed down at thy presence.
For since the beginning of the world men have not heard, nor perceived by the ear, neither hath the eye seen, O God, beside thee, what he hath prepared for him that waiteth for him.
Thou meetest him that rejoiceth and worketh righteousness, those that remember thee in thy ways: *behold, thou art wroth; for we have sinned: in those is continuance, and we shall be saved.*

God is the potter, we are the clay. He made us, not we ourselves. His joy and pleasure is to meet His people, to fellowship with them as a friend, and He wants this more than we want it. But it will be on His terms, not ours. His terms are praise and thanksgiving, a broken and contrite spirit, a joy in Him and His loving sufficiency in all our thoughts and desires. Praise breaks through the darkness every time. Praise breaks through soulish emotion. Loud praise does it faster. Thank you Lord.

Deceiving Spirits
The purpose of a deceiving spirit is to make a person think they are right when, in fact, they are wrong. Deception blinds believers[xvi] from seeing the true will of the Lord, often making them think they really are doing it! Deceiving spirits provide false revelation. The individual, blinded from true revelation from the Lord due to the deceiver, often mis-uses Scripture to justify wrong behavior, and further solidifies it through false prophecy. Although there are many interesting examples in Scripture, Jehoshaphat is particularly fascinating because of the visible connection between emotions and a deceiving spirit.

Jehoshaphat succeeded his father Asa to the throne of Judah. Both Asa and Jehoshaphat helped clear much (albeit not all) the land of idolatry, and saw marvelous successes on the battlefield due to stunning help from the Lord. They reigned a total of 66 years between them. Meanwhile, idolatry was rampant in the remaining ten tribes of Israel. Each king of Israel outdid their predecessor in evil deeds before the Lord, finally winding up with one of the most notorious kings of all – Ahab and his despicable wife, Jezebel. Both Ahab and Jezebel worshipped baal, and murdered God's prophets at will.

One would think that a Godly, faithful king such as Jehoshaphat would have the sense to avoid an Ahab and Jezebel at all costs. Not Jehoshaphat.

2 Chronicles 18:1
*Now Jehoshaphat had riches and honour in abundance, **and joined affinity with Ahab.***

Most common translations of this verse additionally translate affinity with Ahab to mean an alliance by marriage. He married off his son to Ahab's daughter! Would any Christian parent recommend marrying a daughter of Hitler, Stalin, or another such despot? Why would Jehoshaphat be this stupid, particularly in light of God's clear instruction to make no ungodly covenants with heathen nations because of their idolatry (Deuteronomy 7:2; Joshua 23:7-8, et al)? Ahab was clearly an idolater with Jezebel, and Jezebel was a Sidonian, a heathen who served baal.

Marriage to their daughter was an obvious violation of all that Jehoshaphat knew to do, and certainly there were lots of suitable alternatives within Judah.

But Jehoshaphat's emotions were involved.   The particular woman was not the issue, it was the tug at a heart that longed to bring Israel and Judah back together.   Jehoshaphat deeply longed for national reunification, and his emotion overrode his better sense to avoid entangling himself with a sister nation that had forsaken God. We can look back today with hindsight, but we haven't a true understanding of the strong emotional tie Jehoshaphat had via his "roots" and spiritual heritage.   A modern day Messianic Jew has a better feel for the tug Jehoshaphat felt, but even this is a minor comparison to the true depth of his soulish emotion.   Clouded by seemingly Godly justification, Jehoshaphat moved outside of the will of God.

A few years later, Jehoshaphat consented to go to war with Ahab against Syria to regain the lost Israeli city of Ramoth-Gilead. With some inclination still left to consult God before taking military action, Jehoshaphat demanded to hear from a prophet of God (Micaiah) instead of Ahab's proffer of 400 false prophets.

At this point, Jehoshaphat was clearly under the influence of a deceiving spirit. Through Micaiah, God told both Ahab and Jehoshaphat that Ahab would die in the battle. He also told them of the lying spirits the Lord allowed to be placed in the false prophets, and further told them to forget the whole idea of going to war, and instead to go back home in peace. Ignoring the prophet's warning, Jehoshaphat went into battle. He didn't even flinch when Ahab showed up in common soldier attire, leaving Jehoshaphat to be the primary target in kingly battle dress (2 Chronicles 18 and 1 Kings 22)! We're talking about serious spiritual blindness!

What started as a soulish emotional decision to ally with idolatrous Ahab for the purpose of reunifying the homeland later became open deception and disobedience to God's revelation. It takes spiritual deception to make a godly man dumber-than-dirt blind. Lying spirits and deceiving spirits were at work to accomplish the deception.

"But I would never be that stupid today!" Oh no? How many times have we heard that Christians can never become demonized by evil spirits? This very idea comes from a deceiving spirit! Who else would satan endeavor to afflict? How many times have you heard genuine prophets prophecy out of their own souls instead of exclusively by the spirit of the Lord? (If prophecy doesn't fit with Scripture and the inward witness within your own spirit, then the prophecy came either from demons or the prophet's own soul).

I once was counseling an ordained minister whose reaction to a failing marriage was to seek the counsel of a purported Christian of the opposite sex who had been heavily involved with witchcraft, astral projection, and Native American shamanism. While a fully repentant spouse agonized and became impoverished at home, the minister was deceived into thinking the break up was the will of the Lord. Never mind the thief had stolen the marriage, the family, the ministry, and led them into a vicious legal battle, but the deceiving spirit also convinced the offending party through a series of false prophetic encounters that God's will was to become re-married to the new partner and start a new ministry. The proof of all legitimate works of the Lord is spiritual fruit. Fruit was conspicuously absent in this instance.

Fruit of a corrupt tree produces corrupt fruit. How could both Jehoshaphat and this minister be so deceived? They followed their emotions rather than the Lord's clear revelation. This sometimes happens to believers today when they fail to keep a priority on worship and praise to the Lord, and fail to dine at His table daily to both receive and obey the necessary revelation for the day.

The antidote to deception is enlightenment from the Lord. Spending time around His table provides the needed strength and sustenance to make wise decisions. In His presence is joy and peace, light for our paths, and direction that will always bear good spiritual fruit.

Pride

Pride works in close company with a deceiving spirit. A Christian who remains convinced he or she is right when all Scriptural evidence is to the contrary is a person deceived and captivated by pride. With the exception of the wars to take the Promised Land, I can't think of any war in history that has not been fueled by demonic pride. As Proverbs 13:10 indicates, *only by pride cometh contention.* Pride blocks the receipt of the Lord's revelation.

1 Peter 5:5
Likewise, ye younger, submit yourselves unto the elder. Yea, all of you be subject one to another, and be clothed with humility: ***for God resisteth the proud****, and giveth grace to the humble.*

True praisers of the Lord are humble. If an individual wants to develop a longsuit in humility, they will be wise to first develop a longsuit in praise. King David is a vivid example of a humble man. His psalms are an awesome example of the heart of a praiser, even in the midst of turmoil. This is the same man who was called a man after God's own heart! True, he sinned grievously in having Uriah killed and committing adultery with his wife. He let his flesh overcome him, and he was severely punished. Nevertheless, his heart always returned to roost in humility and praise.

Idolatry
Idolatry and God's revelation go together like an ice cube on a hot day in the desert. They aren't found together. But the Christian who stays deceived acquires idols in his or her heart. Anything placed before God, whether a supposed revelation, a prospective mate, a job, or other worldly things will deny that person a seat at the Lord's dinner table. Sometimes the Lord Himself will fight his way through like He did with Balaam, and other times He will witness to someone who could not be reached any other way, such as with the Apostle Paul. But idolatry is not authorized attire for dinners with the Lord.

There is an interesting progression from deception into idolatry. God will give a false revelation to those who persist in their idols! God is willing to accommodate one's idolatry, giving him an answer consistent with their desires. The end of such action is to be cut off from God's people. One might presume this pertains only to Old Testament Israel. However, many people today share such deceptions. Malachi 3:6 declares "I am the Lord, and I change not."

Ezekiel 14:4-9
*Therefore speak unto them, and say unto them, Thus saith the Lord GOD; Every man of the house of Israel that setteth up his idols in his heart, and putteth the stumblingblock of his iniquity before his face, and cometh to the prophet; **I the LORD will answer him that cometh according to the multitude of his idols;***
That I may take the house of Israel in their own heart, because they are all estranged from me through their idols.

Therefore say unto the house of Israel, Thus saith the Lord GOD; Repent, and turn yourselves from your idols; and turn away your faces from all your abominations.

For every one *of the house of Israel, or of the stranger that sojourneth in Israel,* ***which separateth himself from me, and setteth up his idols in his heart****, and putteth the stumblingblock of his iniquity before his face, and cometh to a prophet to inquire of him concerning me; I the LORD will answer him by myself:*

And I will set my face against that man*, and will make him a sign and a proverb, and I will cut him off from the midst of my people; and ye shall know that I am the LORD.*

And if the prophet be deceived when he hath spoken a thing, I the LORD have deceived that prophet*, and I will stretch out my hand upon him, and will destroy him from the midst of my people Israel.*

Fatigue

Battles can be wearisome, and all warriors need rest and good nutrition. Although fatigue is an obvious hindrance to enthusiastic praise and worship, it can be so obvious that it is overlooked in recognizing open doors to demonic attack and deception. Certainly the regularity with which we dine at the Master's table is affected by fatigue. So often the believer schedules around worldly responsibilities rather than around mealtimes with the Lord. As a result, believers sometimes find themselves working longer hours, which can compromise their time with the Father. Allow the Lord to direct your path in work, lest work become a barrier to Him rather than the blessing it should be.

Spiritual Complacency

At first, spiritual dullness and complacency might seem to be the result of any or all of a host of problems including those previously noted.   But more often,   spiritual laziness and complacency are a result of lack of fear of the Lord.

Proverbs 1 and 9 plainly state that the fear of the Lord is the beginning of knowledge and wisdom.   Referring prophetically to Jesus in Isaiah 11: 1-5, the fear of the Lord helped Jesus to avoid judging with his eyes, and reproving from what passed into his ears.[29]

A healthy fear of the Lord helps us today in the same manner – including avoiding the wrong kind of self-focus: self-judgment, self-condemnation, self-disappointment, etc.   But most important, the fear of the Lord helps believers maintain the respect, awe, reverence, and self-abasement before the Lord. Without the fear of the Lord, pride and self-glory arises even over the very relationship the believer seeks to build with Him! A coldness of fellowship replaces the warmth as complacency toward the spirit of knowledge and fear of the Lord (Isaiah 11:2) grows.

My friend and brother in Christ, Rev. Tim Sullivan wrote the following concerning the primacy of walking in the fear of the Lord[xvii]:

It is a grievous error on the part of far too many Christians to cultivate a cavalier and lackadaisical attitude towards their Heavenly Father and the things of God. You may

---

[29] *Isaiah 11:3-4*
And shall make him of quick understanding in the fear of the LORD: and he shall not judge after the sight of his eyes, neither reprove after the hearing of his ears:
But with righteousness shall he judge the poor, and reprove with equity for the meek of the earth: and he shall smite the earth with the rod of his mouth, and with the breath of his lips shall he slay the wicked.

notice this in the way they conduct their personal lives, in the way they worship, and even in the way they address God in prayer.

An intimate relationship with God is a very precious thing, nurtured and developed over time spent in communion with Him, and in learning to do those things that are pleasing in His sight. The same holds true in human relationships, and in human friendships...

What does it mean to live in the "fear of the Lord"? Does it mean we should hide from His presence, as did Adam after his transgression? Should we be afraid to speak to One so Holy, so Powerful, so much better that we, as was Moses when God first spoke to him? Should we live in perpetual terror of being struck down by His Wrath?...

To walk in the fear of the Lord is not to be afraid that He will hurt us or abandon us. It is to walk in the reverence, the respect, and the obedience that is due the Almighty God...It is also to walk circumspectly, knowing that we all shall appear before Him to give account of our conduct as His sons.

When there is no fear of the Lord in your house of worship, your church becomes only a social get-together, a center for gossip and competition amongst the members...Walk in the fear of the Lord, and you will see the Revival you are longing for.

When we walk in the fear of the Lord, we will see a revival in our own hearts also. The fear of the Lord is an essential ingredient not only to avoid spiritual deception, pride, improper soulish emotion, and spiritual complacency, but it provides the basis for communing with the Lord in the first place!

Deception vs. Revelation: How to Discern the Difference

How can an individual build a healthy fear of the Lord? The answer is two fold. First, we are wise to ask for the Lord to give us the same spirit of knowledge and fear of the Lord that was given to Jesus.

Isaiah 11:1-3
And there shall come forth a rod out of the stem of Jesse, and a Branch shall grow out of his roots:
*And the spirit of the LORD shall rest upon him, the spirit of wisdom and understanding, the spirit of counsel and might, **the spirit of knowledge and of the fear of the LORD;***
***And shall make him of quick understanding in the fear of the LORD:** and he shall not judge after the sight of his eyes, neither reprove after the hearing of his ears:*

A second part of building a proper fear of the Lord is to seek for wisdom from the Lord, apply our hearts to grow in His understanding, and seek this wisdom as diligently as the world seeks after money.

Proverbs 2:1-5
My son, if thou wilt receive my words, and hide my commandments with thee;
So that thou incline thine ear unto wisdom, and apply thine heart to understanding;
Yea, if thou criest after knowledge, and liftest up thy voice for understanding;
If thou seekest her as silver, and searchest for her as for hid treasures;
Then shalt thou understand the fear of the LORD, and find the knowledge of God.

As Ecclesiastes concludes, fearing God and keeping His commandments constitute the whole duty of man.[30]

Remember: God does not want His people deceived.   He wants to commune with each of us freely, while satan wants to confuse and corrupt God's telephone lines through deception. An active, reverential awe for the things of God, the purging of soulish emotions through humble and vigorous praise, and daily dining at the Lord's table are all important keys to maintaining an intimate and dynamic relationship with the Lord in which His revelation manna is freely given and received.

---

[30] *Ecclesiastes 12:13-14*

Let us hear the conclusion of the whole matter: Fear God, and keep his commandments: for this is the whole duty of man.

For God shall bring every work into judgment, with every secret thing, whether it be good, or whether it be evil.

Chapter 10

How Can Believers Become Demonized?

I once heard a fellow pastor lament that not a single person in his church didn't have a major ongoing family crisis requiring extensive counseling. My heart ached when I heard this. In response, I was led to mention the impact evil spirits try to play in individual believer's lives. Realizing I was with a group of people who didn't believe that Christians can become demonized, and not wanting to offend them, I shared a personal incident in which one of my own children had recently come home demonized after playing with some unbeliever friends. After the Lord showed me the presence of both a lying and a sultry spirit in my child, I cast them both out in the name of Jesus Christ. The change in my child's behavior was immediate. End of problem – my child was back to being blessed, happy, and bubbling praises to the Lord again as usual.

After sharing the incident to the group I was meeting with, I received an unexpected reaction. Some people, including several ministers, were aghast at the thought that a believer could have a demon. I explained how it can happen that believers can become possessed with a demon. That led to even more discussion – partly because I used the word "possessed" instead of the better, less volatile term of "demonized". But nevertheless, the doctrinal rejection of the thought challenged me to take another look at New Testament incidents of demonized, born again believers.

The questions that perplexed the believers were these: can a born-again believer become demonized? How can holy spirit occupy the same space as an evil spirit? Why are there no records after the day of Pentecost which specifically mention believers becoming demonized/possessed of an evil spirit?

Searching the Scriptures
Some of the answers to these questions are easy to figure out, but documenting them properly from Scripture is not. I want to outline the process the Lord led me through to answer them because as believers reach out to do what Jesus did (preach, teach, and heal), these same questions will arise over and over again. Indeed, the specific reason why many Christian churches are problem-filled instead of Holy Spirit-filled is precisely because where there is lack of knowledge (including this area of demons and how they function against God's people today), people become destroyed.[31] People today are perishing for lack of knowledge in this area right in Christian churches all across America, all across your community, and all across the world.

Let's start by answering these questions in reverse order. Perhaps this will help you help someone else who has been taught that demons can't afflict the born-again believers. The question of whether believers can become demonized may be obvious to some, and offensive to others. There are millions of Christians held captive by this very issue. Pray for the Holy Spirit to lift the scales from the eyes of the Christian church!

---

[31] *Hosea 4:6 - My people are destroyed for lack of knowledge: because thou hast rejected knowledge, I will also reject thee, that thou shalt be no priest to me: seeing thou hast forgotten the law of thy God, I will also forget thy children.*

Why are there no records mentioning believers becoming demonized after Pentecost? Although there are no records applying the terms "possession" or "demonized" after Pentecost, there are three records which clearly show that believers were indeed demonized by evil spirits, and two more which certainly may suggest it. The first one is Ananias and Sapphira in the book of Acts.

Ananias and Sapphira

Acts 5:1-3
But a certain man named Ananias, with Sapphira his wife, sold a possession,
And kept back part of the price, his wife also being privy to it, and brought a certain part, and laid it at the apostles' feet.
*But Peter said, Ananias, **why hath Satan filled thine heart** to lie to the Holy Ghost, and to keep back part of the price of the land?*

Does this record say either Ananias or his wife were possessed or demonized? No. Were they demonized? Yes – satan filling a person's heart certainly works for me to describe a demonized individual. Were these two people born again believers? It doesn't say, but why would they be giving money to the apostles if they weren't? What spirits were involved? Lying and deceiving spirits are indicated, and perhaps there were several others including a spirit of death.

Diotrephes, a Born Again Witch

The next record to note regards Diotrephes. He controlled his congregation. He was what I refer to as a Christian witch because he exerted ungodly control over God's people.

3 John 9-10
I wrote unto the church: but Diotrephes, who loveth to have the
preeminence among them, receiveth us not.
Wherefore, if I come, I will remember his deeds which he
doeth, prating against us with malicious words: and not
content therewith, neither doth he himself receive the
brethren, and forbiddeth them that would, and casteth them
out of the church.

Diotrephes was a leader in the church. He was also acting as a
witch by controlling the walk of other Christians within the
flock. Does it say he was demonized, in this case by a spirit of
pride? No. But was his behavior indicative of a believer who
was? Very clearly yes.

A leader in the church who loves to have the preeminence, who
goes so far as to maliciously slander another believer, who
controls the behavior of people in his congregation, and casts
people out of his church for merely associating with other
ministers in Christ has more than a simple, unsubmitted attitude
of the flesh.

Diotrephes was not a Christian who did not know better, a baby
who has not yet learned to walk in love. His was not the walk
of someone weak in character who decided to sin due to a
simple sinful nature. Diotrephes was the head Christian witch
in his local church! I believe that a spirit of pride deceived him
into working for satan. It opened the door for a spirit of
jealousy to override what should have been joy in Christ at
having the Apostle Paul minister in his church to bless the
Lord's people.

How Can Believers Become Demonized?

1 Timothy 4:1and 2:
Now the Spirit speaketh expressly, that in the latter times *some shall depart from the faith, giving heed to seducing* [deceiving] *spirits, and doctrines of devils* [demons];
Speaking lies in hypocrisy; having their conscience seared with a hot iron;

Diotrephes had departed from the faith – not all of it perhaps, but certainly in this key area of his ministry. Ananias and Sapphira died because they were deceived by demons into thinking they could solicit and manipulate the praise of other Christians by making a show of financial giving. The Christian church needs to know that demons actively try to afflict brethren in order to affect the entire local church. Jesus clearly taught how to get rid of the problem by casting out demons – it's a part of the healing ministry He gave us to operate. A shepherd over a flock must know about these things in order to help guard it. That is why Paul was led by the Lord to write the warning in I Timothy 4 as he did. Clearly, evil spirits can and do afflict the faithful brethren and must be dealt with, not ignored.

What Does it Mean to Become Demonized?
Does "giving heed to seducing spirits" or any other kind of evil spirit constitute becoming possessed or demonized? Is it the same as having satan enter one's heart like he did to Ananias and Sapphira? I cannot provide that answer because I do not know from direct textural language. But the strong inference of Acts 5 suggests a clear affirmative answer.

The demonic mechanisms experienced by Ananias and Sapphira as well as Diotrephes result in severe injury to the church and the individual born again believer. These mechanisms are still operating in the church today. Is it always total possession/demonization? No. Ananias and Sapphira, by all outward appearances to other believers, looked perfectly fine, and for that matter so did Diotrephes. It was by revelation from the Lord that Peter identified and dealt with the demonization of Ananias and Sapphira. It takes revelation to discern demonic influences in the church today too.

Do evil spirits enter in, around, or upon people? How can an evil spirit occupy the same space as Holy Spirit? The Scripture, as far as I know at this time, does not make a distinction. I do not know if an evil spirit can occupy the same space as the Holy Spirit or not. I do know that satan entered the presence of the Lord to accuse Job (Job 1:6-12), and I know from Acts 5:2 that satan *filled the heart* of Ananias and Sapphira. I also know that evil spirits are noted as *coming out of* people in other Scriptural accounts, vexing them, etc. Believers can certainly give heed[xviii] to them in the New Testament.

I personally don't believe an evil spirit can occupy the same place as the Holy Spirit, but this is speculation that makes one feel better doctrinally. But I believe it is very clear from Scripture that born again believers can become demonized, including being variously affected and controlled by evil spirits. I believe this occurs most often in those unsubmitted areas of the individual will. Frankly, when it comes to dealing with evil spirits, Jesus was always aggressive. Since He never bothered to discuss the technicalities of the issue, I'm not going to either. Our job is to cast them out when we find them, not polarize the body with theological discussion. Praise God that Jesus Christ died to bring deliverance to all captives - those of us afflicted physically, spiritually, and mentally (theologically!).

Simon the Sorcerer

The third record of a born again believer becoming demonized is noted in Acts 8:23 regarding Simon the sorcerer. Simon had become born-again under the ministry of Philip the Evangelist.

Acts 8:13
Then Simon himself believed also: and when he was baptized, *he continued with Philip, and wondered, beholding the miracles and signs which were done.*

Great! Simon got born again! But Simon had a problem. Acts 8:23 declares he was poisoned by bitterness, and bound by iniquity (NKJV). This occurred *after* he became born again in verse 8:13. The cause for seduction from truth is always demons, for Paul told us in Ephesians 6:12 and 13 that we are not contending with flesh and blood but with demonic forces. Denying how these forces endeavor to affect and control believers is a repudiation of one of Paul's main points in the sixth chapter of Ephesians.

What spirits cause (or influence) this type of behavior in believers? Consider how the spirit of bondage affects believers, keeping them from having an intimate relationship with the Lord.[32] For example, how do the false prophets of I John 4:1,[33] whose spirits are to be tested, get into the New Testament church in the first place? They can first get born-again like any other believer, then become seduced by deceiving spirits into false prophetic utterance which then upsets their local church.

---

[32] *Romans 8:15 - For ye have not received the spirit of bondage again to fear; but ye have received the Spirit of adoption, whereby we cry, Abba, Father.*
[33] *I John 4:1 - Beloved, believe not every spirit, but try the spirits whether they are of God: because many false prophets are gone out into the world.*

Evil Spirits Departed

A final record must be reviewed in Acts chapter 19, the section on Paul's extraordinary miracles.

Acts 19:11-12
And God wrought special miracles by the hands of Paul:
So that from his body were brought unto the sick handkerchiefs
*or aprons, and the diseases departed from them, **and the evil***
spirits went out of them.

Evil spirits went out of people whom Paul ministered to, and the record in Acts 19:12 declares that evil spirits went out from those who used the handkerchiefs that he anointed. Were all those people unbelievers from whom evil spirits departed? Highly doubtful. Consider how many unbelievers flocked into your church last Sunday who might be disposed to take a handkerchief that your minister had anointed. Is it not logical to recognize the probability that these healings and deliverance from evil spirits were mostly among believers and their family and friends? But somehow the mere mention of believers being afflicted with evil spirits is summarily rejected across much of Christianity today.

Acts 5:14-16
And believers were the more added to the Lord, multitudes
both of men and women.
*Insomuch that **they** brought forth the sick into the streets, and*
laid them on beds and couches, that at the least the shadow of
Peter passing by might overshadow some of them.
There came also a multitude out of the cities round about unto
*Jerusalem, bringing sick folks, **and them which were vexed***
***with unclean spirits**: and they were healed every one.*

The result of the awe and respectful fear of the Lord that arose among the believers after the death of Ananias and Sapphira is recorded in Acts 5:14 – multitudes of believers were added to the Lord. Thereafter, multitudes of believing men and women took their sick to be healed. Another multitude from the cities also took their sick and demonically afflicted (vexed[xix] by unclean spirits) for healing. Is it not logical to presume that many of this additional multitude of people from the cities and those they brought were also believers?

Let me ask a question. Do Christians ever get sick today? If they still get sick today despite the fact that Jesus paid for their sickness, and healed them by His stripes, then there must be more to receiving one's healing than simply assuming healing either 1) will occur automatically at the new birth (which certainly does happen frequently but not always), or 2) that it is not God's will to be healed (which is a clear violation of III John 2's statement that it is God's will that all people prosper and be in health even as their souls prosper).

Just as sickness has not gone away from among the Christian church, neither has demonization of believers gone away. The victory over both must be claimed with the *exousia* authority given to the Church, and received in faith from Jesus Christ. The argument that believers cannot become demonized today makes as much Biblical sense as saying that believers can never get sick.[xx]

Staying Balanced
The field of demonology in the church gets either too little attention, as in the case of many afflicted churches today, or it can get too much, especially during one's initial learning curve when the subject seems repulsively overwhelming. But remember, Hosea 4:6 says that God's people become destroyed

for lack of knowledge. The Apostle Paul's instruction in Ephesians strikes the proper balance – neither minimizing the seriousness of the problem, nor overemphasizing it.

Ephesians 6:10-13
Finally, my brethren, be strong in the Lord, and in the power of his might.
*Put on the whole armour of God, **that ye may be able to stand against the wiles of the devil.***
For we wrestle not against flesh and blood, but against principalities, against powers, against the rulers of the darkness of this world, against spiritual wickedness in high places.
*Wherefore take unto you the whole armour of God, **that ye may be able to withstand in the evil day,** and having done all, to stand.*

The evil day is already here. Satan and his demons have many more years of experience attacking through holes of sin, unholiness, generational curses, etc. in the believer's armor than you or I have in claiming the blood of Jesus. Clearly it is the individual believer's job to grow up and learn how to plug these holes under the instruction and tutelage of the Lord and the fellowship of the saints.

Jesus Christ delivered us from the authority (*exousia*) of darkness.[34] Yet, like the healing He also provided through His stripes, believers must claim their deliverance against demonic afflictions. Just as Joshua's conquest of the Promised Land was not automatic, neither is a believer's deliverance automatic until

---

[34] *Colossians 1:13*
Who hath delivered us from the power of darkness, and hath translated us into the kingdom of his dear Son:

he or she applies the Lord's revelation in Scripture, and any additional *rhema* He may give for the situation.

1 Peter 5:8-9
Be sober, be vigilant; because your adversary the devil, as a roaring lion, walketh about, seeking whom he may devour:
*Whom resist stedfast in the faith, **knowing that the same afflictions are accomplished in your brethren that are in the world.***

We are to be sober and vigilant except when it comes to admitting that demons can directly influence your church and your behavior. Excuse me? The very same evil spirits which caused the cases of possession that Jesus dealt with, Paul and Peter, and many other believers encountered in the early church are alive and well around believers today who deny their influence and existence. We have weak, problem-filled churches because we have weak understanding of our Biblical authority. It is our responsibility to aggressively deal with satan and his principalities, powers, rulers of darkness, and wicked spirits in high places. I am told that a substantial number of people in mental institutions are born again Christians who suffer from demonic afflictions that war against the soul. It is long past time to wake up the sleeping church.

Praise God for His goodness to help us open our eyes to the power of His blood and the instruction of His Word to help us put on the armor He so lovingly supplies to help us stand against the wiles of the devil. Let us spend time each day at His table, growing up into Him as a people zealous to repent and hungry to learn from the Master teacher. Let us speak to Him, but more importantly, let us *listen* to His revelation manna. May we obediently respond to His voice; our great Shepherd speaks to the sheep of His pasture.

Remember: Believers are prime targets for demonic influence. Jesus taught His disciples how to deal with them. By revelation they can be detected and cast out. Although you don't need revelation to smash a mosquito, demons are nevertheless similar - an annoyance that is far smaller than believers tend to think, but also far more pervasive than most of us realize. Demons can be dealt with using the authority of Jesus Christ, and they must obey in His name. Become confident of the Lord's revelation, and dealing with demons becomes a far simpler matter.

Ephesians chapter six clearly shows that believers can learn to stand strong in the Lord if they are willing to pay the price to stand in the power of His might. The power of His might comes from using the armor He gives. He'll teach how to use it by revelation-manna. Why not ask Him how?

Chapter 11

The Way of the Lord

Some years ago I was rock climbing in one of the southwestern states. A hundred feet off the ground or so, I reached an impasse. I had found a semi-comfortable perch on a slightly inverted slope, but I could go no further. There were no handholds or leg holds within sight to advance any further, and because of the inverted angle of the rock face, it took effort just to cling there without falling.

I asked God for help. Quickly a reply came, "Lunge up to the right." Suddenly I had a faith problem. Do I believe the revelation the Lord gave me and lunge as He directed, knowing that to do so I would have to forsake my quasi-safe position? There was no way to recover the perch once I left it. I couldn't re-trace my way back down, and the effort to remain in position was too arduous to linger for long. I had only two choices – stay where I was until I fell, or trust the word of the Lord.

I elected to obey the Lord. With what strength remained, I lunged up toward the right. My hand landed on a small invisible prominent of rock that had been just beyond both my sight and reach. Grabbing onto it enabled me to complete the climb successfully. The Lord showed me the way by revelation, and taught me a valuable lesson in trusting His voice.

Jesus Said "I Am The Way"

Consider the phrase, "The way of the Lord." The way of the Lord is something that is definable.

John 14:6
*Jesus saith unto him, **I am the way, the truth, and the life**: no man cometh unto the Father, but by me.*

"The way of the Lord" is an often-used phrase in the Bible, particularly in the Old Testament. It is often assumed to mean the behavior of the Lord or the behavior His people are supposed to have. Rarely is it ever defined any more precisely. It is presumed to be a broad, somewhat vague term referring to Biblical behavior in general rather than to any specific action. But God's Word is not vague. It uses words specifically, with specific intent. "The way of the Lord" has a very specific character.

Defining the Way of the Lord

We need to know what the way of the Lord is. We need to learn how to find it, and how to stay on it. Let's begin by finding out what it is.

Genesis 18:16-19
And the men rose up from thence, and looked toward Sodom: and Abraham went with them to bring them on the way.
And the LORD said, Shall I hide from Abraham that thing which I do;
Seeing that Abraham shall surely become a great and mighty nation, and all the nations of the earth shall be blessed in him?
*For I know him, that he will command his children and his household after him, **and they shall keep the way of the LORD**, to do justice and judgment; that the LORD may bring upon Abraham that which he hath spoken of him.*

Sodom and Gomorrah were spiritually dark places. By way of revelation, the Lord talked with Abraham, revealing what He was going to do to these cities which were almost completely given over to idolatry, homosexuality, and ungodliness. In these verses in Genesis 18, the Lord is talking about giving revelation, reasoning that Abraham will be faithful to not only utilize this revelation (i.e. this "way") but pass it on to his children and household as well.

God said that Abraham would *"keep the way* [the revelation] *of the Lord to do justice and judgment."* Why? So that the Lord could bring to pass the prior revelation regarding Abraham becoming the father of many nations.

So often we presume "the way of the Lord" refers to the written Scripture. But this incident with Abraham predates written Scripture. Moses is credited with writing down the Genesis account, and Moses was many hundreds of years still in the future. Clearly, the "way of the Lord" of Genesis 18:19 has nothing to do with a broad, generalized manner of behavior. It has to do with a very specific revelation that was given to Abraham.

Often the first or early usages of a word or phrase in the Bible defines it. The Hebrew word for "the way" is *derek*, meaning a road. Used figuratively of the Lord, it refers to a course of action. But in context, it is not just any course of action. In this case, the way of the Lord is in reference to action upon spoken revelation, God to Abraham. For Abraham to keep the way of the Lord was to perform the specific revelation God gave him.

In Exodus, the Word of God continues to define the way of the Lord in the record concerning the wilderness wandering.

Exodus 13:17-22
*And it came to pass, when Pharaoh had let the people go, that God led them not through **the way of the land of the Philistines**, although that was near; for God said, Lest peradventure the people repent when they see war, and they return to Egypt:*
***But God led the people about, through the way of the wilderness of the Red sea:** and the children of Israel went up harnessed out of the land of Egypt.*
And Moses took the bones of Joseph with him: for he had straitly sworn the children of Israel, saying, God will surely visit you; and ye shall carry up my bones away hence with you.
And they took their journey from Succoth, and encamped in Etham, in the edge of the wilderness.
*And the LORD went before them by day in a pillar of a cloud, **to lead them the way;** and by night in a pillar of fire, to give them light; to go by day and night:*
He took not away the pillar of the cloud by day, nor the pillar of fire by night, from before the people.

The easier and shorter route to the Promised Land was through the land of the Philistines. But God did not choose this route at all. Instead, He chose a different path, leading them by supernatural means – a pillar of a cloud by day, and of fire by night. There is a greater implication here than just a physical pathway to get to a destination. God's true destination was more than geographical (the Promised Land). It was spiritual. He was trying to get His people to outgrow their complaining spirit (a curse from Egypt), and learn His way (the way of revelation-dependence upon Him).

Deuteronomy 8:1-3
All the commandments which I command thee this day shall ye observe to do, that ye may live, and multiply, and go in and

possess the land which the LORD sware unto your fathers.
*And thou shalt remember all **the way which the LORD thy God
led thee these forty years in the wilderness**, to humble thee, and
to prove thee, to know what was in thine heart, whether thou
wouldest keep his commandments, or no.*
*And he humbled thee, and suffered thee to hunger, and fed thee
with manna, which thou knewest not, neither did thy fathers
know; **that he might make thee know that man doth not live by
bread only, but by every word that proceedeth out of the
mouth of the LORD doth man live.***

The reason God required Israel to wander in the wilderness was
to teach them how to live by revelation. Learning to live by
revelation is a process that requires testing the heart's
commitment to the Lord.

Once again, remember that the exodus and subsequent
wandering occurred prior to the Bible being written. The "every
word" that God's people were to live by were the words of
revelation from the mouth of the Lord. As noted earlier in
chapters five and ten, Jesus quoted Deuteronomy 8:3 to the
devil in Matthew 4:4 when He stated that man will not live by
bread alone, but by every *rhema*, every inspired word of
revelation, that proceeds from the Lord's mouth.

It is revelation-manna that enables God's people to stop
wandering in their wildernesses! Hearing and obeying
revelation *is* the way of the Lord! This is what God so earnestly
tried to get His people to do for over forty years! He even made
it easier by additionally giving them the pillars of cloud and fire
as visual aids!

Psalms 95:6-10
O come, let us worship and bow down: let us kneel before the
LORD our maker.
For he is our God; and we are the people of his pasture, and the
sheep of his hand. **To day if ye will hear his voice,**
Harden not your heart, as in the provocation, and as in the
day of temptation in the wilderness:
When your fathers tempted me, proved me, and saw my work.
Forty years long was I grieved with this generation, and said, It
is a people that do err in their heart, **and they have not known**
my ways:

The hardness of Israel's heart prevented them from hearing the
voice of the Lord. Thus they could not get to know His way of
giving specific revelation. The deliverance from the Egyptian
chariots should have softened them up. The daily provision of
manna from heaven should have been a clue, and the over-
eating plague of quail after complaining to the Lord about the
manna should have been a wake-up call. The pillar of the
cloud and fire might have told even the most eminently prideful
among them that the Lord wanted them to learn to depend on
"the way" of His voice to them.

Today we don't need pillars of smoke and fire. Today, in
contrast to the days of Moses, we have the same full measure of
the gift of holy spirit that Jesus Christ has. Though dramatic
visual aides like these pillars are nice to have, when we are led
by the powerful Spirit of the Living Christ, we don't often need
them. However, the same prideful independence that
characterized Israel in the wilderness (i.e. in their resistance to
the leading of the Lord) still characterizes man today. People
still fail to gather the Lord's manna each day.

The Way of the Lord

Romans 8:13-14
For if ye live after the flesh, ye shall die: but if ye through the Spirit do mortify the deeds of the body, ye shall live.
For as many as are led by the Spirit of God, they are the sons of God.

The flesh wars against the Spirit. When people are walking by fleshly information, they cannot walk by the Spirit-provided words from the mouth of the Lord. Israel preferred to walk by their fleshly information – their own eyes, ears, fears, and ideas. When we learn to hear information from the Spirit and rely on it, we can grow to become led by it. The words we receive into our spirit from the Lord are the words of revelation manna that we are to live and govern our lives by. This is the way of the Lord.

What the Way of the Lord is Not
The record of Moses receiving the ten commandments from God is a wonderful testimony of what the way of the Lord is. While on the mountain, Moses received revelation on what was going on down in the camp. Here we see what the way of the Lord is not.

Exodus 32:1, 7-8
And when the people saw that Moses delayed to come down out of the mount, the people gathered themselves together unto Aaron, and said unto him, Up, make us gods, which shall go before us; for as for this Moses, the man that brought us up out of the land of Egypt, we wot not what is become of him.

And the LORD said unto Moses, Go, get thee down; **for thy people, which thou broughtest out of the land of Egypt, have corrupted themselves:**

They have turned aside quickly out of the way which I commanded them: they have made them a molten calf, and have worshipped it, and have sacrificed thereunto, and said, These be thy gods, O Israel, which have brought thee up out of the land of Egypt.

Revelation from the Lord in times of distress is very comforting, and God has no shortage of words to give. But refusal to seek the Lord to get our revelation-manna distinguishes the Aarons from the Moses' of this world. The Lord has *His way* for each individual, and we must seek to learn it and become reliant upon it. Aaron could have asked the Lord for help to learn how to deal with the complaints of the people. But instead, Aaron determined that he could fill the need, and show the people another way. Lack of reliance on the Lord's way of revelation manna for the situation at hand was quickly replaced by fleshly self-reliance with obvious help from evil spirits.

Did the gods of Egypt bring deliverance to Israel or did one man's obedience to the Lord's revelation, the way of the Lord, bring it about? There is no question that the Lord's way is the way of hearing and obeying words that proceed out of His mouth. This is still today how God's people are to live, for as Malachi 3:6a declares in the context of disobedience to His revelation ordinances, *I am the LORD, I change not.*

When a person sins, what happens? They interrupt their spiritual connection, like a telephone that goes dead in the middle of a conversation. The ability to hear revelation becomes disconnected. The means for the communication is not lost, but temporarily the phone line is disconnected. Sin turns people aside, disconnecting the communication link for a season until the sin is confessed and cleansed, and righteousness is restored (I John 1:9). The way of the Lord is the way of receiving communications from the Lord and then obeying them. Sin, such as worshipping the golden calf and other false idols, is not the way of the Lord. The way of the Lord is being led by the Spirit of the living God through revelation from Him.

Find the Way by Hearing His Voice
Moses well understood how to submit, acquire, and obey revelation from God. There is nothing secret about the Lord's desire and willingness to provide "the way of the Lord" for each of us today. There is nothing to prevent us from doing as Moses did to join the Lord in His meeting place to find His way daily.

Exodus 33:11-14
And the LORD spake unto Moses face to face, as a man speaketh unto his friend. *And he turned again into the camp: but his servant Joshua, the son of Nun, a young man, departed not out of the tabernacle.*
And Moses said unto the LORD, See, thou sayest unto me, Bring up this people: and thou hast not let me know whom thou wilt send with me. Yet thou hast said, I know thee by name, and thou hast also found grace in my sight.
Now therefore, I pray thee, if I have found grace in thy sight, **shew me now thy way, that I may know thee,** *that I may find grace in thy sight: and consider that this nation is thy people.*
And he said, My presence shall go with thee, *and I will give thee rest.*

The way of the Lord is not hard to find. Jesus Christ did not make access difficult. Quite the opposite - He made it easy.

Revelation 3:20-22
Behold, I stand at the door, and knock: **if any man hear my voice, and open the door, I will come in to him, and will sup with him, and he with me.**

To him that overcometh will I grant to sit with me in my throne, even as I also overcame, and am set down with my Father in his throne.
He that hath an ear, let him hear what the Spirit saith unto the churches.

The way of the Lord is found by entering His presence, and hearing His words of revelation manna. All that Moses did, and all that anyone who wants to work for God must do, is learn to enter the presence of the Lord, and find out from His lips which way He wants them to go.   Moses learned to cultivate a speaking and listening relationship with the Lord. So must we if we would walk in the way of the Lord.

The Lord will work in marvelous ways with each one of us as we grow to faithfully come into His presence, and stay long enough to hear His voice.   Anything less puts us in league with Aaron, walking in our own sparks, thereby following a new way - the way of the flesh.

We must have revelation from the Lord to know and do His will. Our most difficult work is often not in carrying out the revelation received. We tend to be good at doing things. But we must become good at doing the things *He specifically asks* us to do. The most difficult thing for most people is to wait upon the Lord to find out their next assignment. We want to take matters into our own hands, like the idolators of the camp who couldn't wait for Moses to return. When we refuse to dine at the Lord's table for our assignments, we build golden calves for ourselves.

Our primary work should be the work of listening to His voice, and getting clear on His way for our day. Our primary work therefore is the work of praise and worship upon our knees (or singing and dancing!) before Him to hear what He wants to tell us. Praise God for His loving kindness and mercy to allow us to come boldly before Him as Moses, Abraham, Peter, John, Paul, Philip, and so many others who learned to find the way of the Lord.

Finding The Way of the Lord in the Sanctuary
The way of the Lord is found in His sanctuary.

Psalms 77:11-13
I will remember the works of the LORD: surely I will remember thy wonders of old.
I will meditate also of all thy work, and talk of thy doings.
Thy way, O God, is in the sanctuary: *who is so great a God as our God?*

God's way is in the sanctuary because it is there that we most often hear His counsel. Jesus is the minister of the sanctuary.[35] This is where we dine with Him at His table! The sanctuary is a very special place, a place of reverence in the Old Testament, a place to take off one's shoes and come before the Minister of the sanctuary today – Jesus, our King.

Leviticus 19:30
*Ye shall keep my sabbaths, and **reverence my sanctuary:** I am the LORD.*

---

[35] *Hebrews 8:1-2*
Now of the things which we have spoken this is the sum: We have such an high priest, who is set on the right hand of the throne of the Majesty in the heavens;
A minister of the sanctuary, and of the true tabernacle, which the Lord pitched, and not man.

Psalms 134:2
Lift up your hands in the sanctuary, and bless the LORD

Psalms 150:1
Praise ye the LORD. **Praise God in his sanctuary:** *praise him in the firmament of his power*

Hebrews 8:1-2
Now of the things which we have spoken this is the sum: We have such an high priest, who is set on the right hand of the throne of the Majesty in the heavens;
A minister of the sanctuary, and of the true tabernacle, which the Lord pitched, and not man.

God always wanted His people to follow His specific revelation to them individually. Collectively, they would be one people because they would be hearing one voice, from one source, though it would be heard individually. Israel rejected this privilege as individuals, choosing instead to selectively listen to God's priests. These priests, the Levites, did not remain faithful to their call to minister in the sanctuary. God then selected the house of Zadok out from among the Levites to retain the privilege of hearing from Him in the sanctuary. Today in Jesus Christ, our access to the sanctuary – the place where we learn to hear the way of the Lord by revelation – has been given.

The Bible declares of itself that it is the truth[36] and it also declares it is life to all who hear it. But only Jesus declared that He is the way. Why? Because "the way" is the "path" of receiving revelation from Him. The way of revelation is found in the sanctuary, of which Jesus is the attendant high priest. Hence Jesus, as the living Word in the flesh, is the truth and the

---

[36] *John 17:17 Sanctify them through thy truth:* **thy word is truth.**

life. Because of the revelation He gives us, He is also the Way. The Lord's way is revelation to His people.

In chapter seven we saw that every great accomplishment of faith listed in Hebrews chapter 11 was preceded by the receipt of specific revelation from the Lord. The recipients exercised faith to hold onto, believe, and carry out the revelation they received. Their way was the way of walking by revelation, with faith in revelation not in their eyesight. This is the faith without which it is impossible to please God.[37]

Committing Your Way to Him

Understanding that "the way of the Lord" pertains to being led by revelation from the Lord, and also that faith is the action upon that revelation, certain familiar verses take on a new light.

Psalms 37:4-9
Delight thyself also in the LORD; and he shall give thee the desires of thine heart.
Commit thy way unto the LORD; trust also in him; and he shall bring it to pass.
And he shall bring forth thy righteousness as the light, and thy judgment as the noonday.
*Rest in the LORD, and wait patiently for him: **fret not thyself because of him who prospereth in his way**, because of the man who bringeth wicked devices to pass.*
Cease from anger, and forsake wrath: fret not thyself in any wise to do evil.
*For evildoers shall be cut off: **but those that wait upon the LORD, they shall inherit the earth**.*

---

[37]*Hebrews 11:6 - **But without faith it is impossible to please him:** for he that cometh to God must believe that he is, and that he is a rewarder of them that diligently seek him.*

God has often done exceedingly above all that we ask or think to bless us, and each one of us can recount several examples. But no where does He guarantee doing so. However, the things He does guarantee doing are those things that He first gives by revelation.

Committing our way is a good example. Not every way of ours is pleasing and acceptable to the Lord. But His way - His revelation given to us which we have seen is literally "the way of the Lord" for us – this is "the way" He means for us to commit to Him. We are to trust this word by faith and live by it as words of life proceeding from His mouth. He will absolutely bring them to pass. If we develop a lifestyle of waiting on Him for these words, learning His way from His lips, we shall inherit the earth.

"Commit" means to roll upon, to give it to the Lord. To commit our way to the Lord is not talking about committing our fleshly way to God, then requesting God to honor it in prayer. Verse 5 is not saying, "God, this is the way I want to go and I commit it to You, Lord." This verse is talking about learning the Lord's way from Him by revelation, delighting ourselves in it, and He will perform it when we give it back to Him and say, "Holy Spirit, help me do what the Lord just told me to do." That is what this verse is talking about - committing our way, the way that He revealed to us - back to Him. Then by faith in that word of revelation, we trust Him to bring it to pass.

Why does it work this way? Because we are dealing with revelation from the King. If we are faithful to carry out precisely as the King says, He will back up our faith action. Thereby will He bring forth our righteousness as the light and our judgment as the noonday.

He'll Teach Our Hands To War

God's way works in every situation. Joshua conquered Jericho by obeying revelation. He lost the next battle against the city of Ai because he didn't bother to seek revelation. He succeeded only when he sought and obeyed the way of the Lord - His specific situational revelation for the attack. The Lord will teach us to war if we learn to hear His voice like David did.

Psalms 18:28-34

For thou wilt light my candle: the LORD my God will enlighten my darkness.

For by thee I have run through a troop; and by my God have I leaped over a wall.

As for God, his way is perfect: the word of the LORD is tried: he is a buckler to all those that trust in him.

For who is God save the LORD? or who is a rock save our God?

It is God that girdeth me with strength, and maketh my way perfect.

He maketh my feet like hinds' feet, and setteth me upon my high places.

He teacheth my hands to war, so that a bow of steel is broken by mine arms.

Biblically speaking, "light" often refers to revelation from God. This familiar passage is not talking about reading the Bible to get instruction on how to conquer an enemy. It is talking about receiving specific situational revelation. God gave David revelation knowledge to wage war against his enemies. "He will light your candle" means that He will give you revelation. The revelation word of the Lord is perfect. It is what we are to live by which proceeds out of His mouth. He is a buckler (i.e. a shield) because of the revelation He gives us in His sanctuary around His table. He teaches us like He taught David – through words. His preferred method for teaching is through words into our spirit.[xxi]

Psalms 25:9
*The meek will he guide in judgment: and **the meek will he teach his way.***

The Bible declares that Moses was the meekest man in all the earth. If the Lord will teach the meek and if He teaches by revelation, then it stands to reason that a man like Moses would receive staggering revelation. The Lord's way is the way of giving revelation manna to feed the meek. We want to always stay meek to the Lord, dining at His table as often as possible.

Now, we don't automatically say "Okay, I'm going to get meek." We develop meekness. First we determine a desire to become meek. Next, we ask the Holy Spirit to help us become more meek, and we trust Him to begin working to help us get there – His way, not our way. The meek are the ones that get down on their knees and praise Him. The meek are the ones that seek Him with their whole heart. The meek are the ones that recognize that without Jesus Christ, they can do nothing. The meek are the ones that constantly go to Him and learn to rely on Him, so that He can show them the way.

Training Our Children
God's way is the way of leadership by revelation. It is also what He wants His children to learn from their parents.

Proverbs 22:6
Train up a child in the way *he should go: and when he is old, he will not depart from it.*

178

Training up children has been done rather poorly over the years. Many Christian parents begin training their children using watered down Bible stories, turning them over to Sunday school teachers for more of the same up through the formative years. With no substance other than stories, and perhaps a few Bible verses committed to memory, no wonder the pressures of the world become more entangling to Christian children's' hearts than the things of God.

The way we are to train up children is not simple exposure to filtered Scripture. The way meant in Proverbs 22:6 is the way of the Lord, meaning the way of receiving revelation from Him. Children are to be trained to enter His gates with thanksgiving and His courts with praise. They are to be trained to enter His sanctuary, open the door to His knock and learn to dine at His table. They are to listen to His voice as He talks with them. This is the way we are to train up our children![xxii]

Our children will not depart from staying close to the lips of the Lord, waiting on Him, and learning to respond with joy to His slightest whisper into their hearts. Drugs? Worldly temptations? Peer pressure? Pornography? Television violence? Video games and addictions? How can these things compare to the attractiveness and thrill of hearing the Lord's still small voice?

If we will train our children to rejoice in His voice to them, they will avoid many of the "growing pains" (lusts) experienced by the world. How much easier it is to resist the delights of the world when we experience the pleasure of His presence. Teaching our children to be led by the Spirit is what God is talking about when He exhorted His people to train up their children in the way.

Narrow is The Way

Walking by revelation manna garnered from the table of the Lord is a narrow walk. It requires discipline, hunger for the Lord, and obedience. This narrow way is not obscure, but there is a price to pay to find it.

Matthew 7:13-14
Enter ye in at the strait gate: for wide is the gate, and broad is the way, that leadeth to destruction, and many there be which go in thereat:
*Because strait is the gate, **and narrow is the way, which leadeth unto life**, and few there be that find it.*

Narrow is the walk by revelation. Why? Well, it's not hard to find, but it requires meekness. It requires the desire to seek the Lord. It requires the desire to praise and worship Him, to enter His gates with thanksgiving, His courts with praise and make these a lifestyle. We then make it a lifestyle to walk by *His* pathway, not ours. The narrow way of the Lord is a walk of dependency, of faithful reliance on Him.

The prideful find this way to be narrow, hard, and obscure. The prideful will say "God gave us a brain and expects us to use it", as if seeking to receive and obey revelation from the Creator of the universe is somehow the opposite of thinking. I personally would have a hard time making such a statement as this to Moses, Noah, Elijah, Jesus, or the Apostle Paul!

The fact is, we are to use our brains to give Him glory His way, not ours. We glorify Him when we do His works through obedience to His *rhema.*[38]

---

[38] *John 15:7-8*
If ye abide in me, and my words abide in you, ye shall ask what ye will, and it shall be done unto you.

The Way of the Lord

The way of the revelation walk is indeed narrow, and few find it because few are willing to surrender themselves. Jesus is embraced by many, but fewer embrace and trust the Holy Spirit whose job is to help and guide them to find the way of dependence on Jesus' manna. Fewer still learn to discipline themselves to linger in His presence to hear.

Oh what a Lord and Savior we have! What a privilege He gave us by His blood! What free access we have to come boldly before His throne of grace when we do it His way, and stay hungry for more of Him!

The Way of John the Baptist

The Scriptures tell us that John the Baptist's job was to prepare the way of the Lord. What was this way and how did he do it?

Matthew 3:1-3
In those days came John the Baptist, preaching in the wilderness of Judaea,
And saying, Repent ye: for the kingdom of heaven is at hand.
For this is he that was spoken of by the prophet Esaias, saying,
*The voice of one crying in the wilderness, **Prepare ye the way of the Lord**, make his paths straight.*

One of the purposes of John the Baptist was to prepare the way of the Lord. What is the way of the Lord? What was John trying to do? What was John's purpose? Repentance. John's purpose was to get the people to repent. What's the purpose of repentance? Specifically it is relationship. It is to clean up the obstacles that sever the relationship between God and man.

Herein is my Father glorified, that ye bear much fruit; so shall ye be my disciples.

Repentance cleans us up so that the relationship can be established and/or restored.

What is the purpose of a relationship with the Lord? So that we can have a fellowship, a close family relationship with God. After one becomes born again, the way to build a growing relationship is to learn what the way of the Lord is. We learn the truth and we receive life from reading the Scriptures. They point us to Jesus, and continually help us become stronger for Him as good food for the soul. But we learn *the way of revelation* from interacting with Jesus, learning how to eat revelation manna from His table. Remember from Chapter Two, Jesus builds His church on revelation.

Jesus Demonstrated the Way of the Lord
Matthew 22:15-16
Then went the Pharisees, and took counsel how they might entangle him in his talk.
*And they sent out unto him their disciples with the Herodians, saying, Master, we know that thou art true, **and teachest the way of God in truth**, neither carest thou for any man: for thou regardest not the person of men.*

The Pharisees and Herodians both voiced that Jesus Christ was teaching the subject of how to have a relationship with God. Nevertheless, they were offended at this prospect, and they rejected the Messiah. However, some of them at least understood that Jesus was trying to teach them about how to have a relationship with God. Nevertheless they were rankled at Jesus' frequent declaration that He spoke the words (*rhema*) of revelation that were given to Him by the Father.[39] The way of

---

[39] *John 17:8 For I have given unto them the words which thou gavest me; and they have received them, and have known surely that I came out from thee, and they have believed that thou didst send me.*

God is the same way heralded in the wilderness by Moses, and by John the Baptist in preparation for the Lord's first appearance. It is the same way heralded by the end times Elijah prophets – the way of walking by revelation from the Lord.

The Way of Thieves and Robbers
John 10:1-6
Verily, verily, I say unto you, **He that entereth not**
by the door into the sheepfold, but climbeth up some other
way, the same is a thief and a robber.
But he that entereth in by the door is the shepherd of the
sheep.
To him the porter openeth; and the sheep hear his voice: and
he calleth his own sheep by name, and leadeth them out.
And when he putteth forth his own sheep, he goeth before
them, and the sheep follow him: for they know his voice.
And a stranger will they not follow, but will flee from him: for
they know not the voice of strangers.
This parable spake Jesus unto them: but they understood not
what things they were which he spake unto them.

This dialogue went over the heads of the disciples. Jesus was talking about maintaining a conversational, two-way relationship with His people. *His way* is through a talking relationship with His people. They know His voice personally. He calls them by name. He'll call you by name in your secret place too as you dine at His table.

But there are robbers and thieves. These can be the religious hierarchy who talk Bible verses but who do not feed at the Lord's table. They will follow the Bible like the Pharisees did,[40] but will not discern and follow the way of the Lord through hearing His voice. There is a remarkable difference. One walks by the Spirit, the other by sight. One has established a personal friendship by learning to enter Jesus' sanctuary. The other has not. One is an active, ongoing mentoring, the other is presumptuously intellectual. One is intimate with the source of life, the other tries to dissect it from a distance.

Only the Holy Spirit can lead a person into the sanctuary. But robbers and thieves characteristically reject intimacy with the Shepherd. Examples typical of our day include the rejection of the availability of the Holy Spirit and His gifts. In essence, robbers and thieves have not met Jesus. Although they may often call out to Him, they'll get no response.

This condition of not hearing the Master's voice must change, or the flocks shepherded by such ministers will be ravaged and dysfunctional, full of carnality. Carnal congregations are the result of leadership which does not feed at the Lord's table continually to learn His way. Repentance can change this condition quickly. This is the message to the seven churches of Revelation chapters two and three.

Ministers who have not learned to hear the sound of the Lord's voice are thieves and robbers. With repentance this situation can change immediately. The first criteria for being a shepherd over a flock is to be able to hear the Chief Shepard's voice. We must first become sheep, learn to feed from His pasture, and go into His sheepfold of protection.

---

[40] *John 5:39 - Search the scriptures; for in them ye think ye have eternal life: and they are they which testify of me.*

The Way of the Lord

I know this situation very well. I used to be a pastor who prayed many one-way prayers. Even though I was ordained a minister of the Gospel of Jesus Christ, I did not know the sound of His voice to me. By His mercy, He has since led me to such a place. How many people have I hurt by not helping them to feed from the table of the Lord? How many of my former pastoral efforts failed to discern the attacks of wolves, and how many wonderful believers were ravaged as a result? I shudder to think, and I have sincerely repented before His throne.

A sheep that has not learned to hear the Shepherd's voice will not hear the call to come out of the pasture where the wolves roam at night. No congregation should be subjected to such risk. If a person does not know the Lord's way of receiving revelation-manna, they will find their own way - the way of non-revelation, religious flesh.

To make sure His disciples got this message clearly, the Lord stated it again.

John 10:7-17
Then said Jesus unto them again, Verily, verily, I say unto you, I am the door of the sheep.
All that ever came before me are thieves and robbers: but the sheep did not hear them.
I am the door: by me if any man enter in, he shall be saved, and shall go in and out, and find pasture.
The thief cometh not, but for to steal, and to kill, and to destroy: I am come that they might have life, and that they might have it more abundantly.
I am the good shepherd: the good shepherd giveth his life for the sheep.

185

But he that is an hireling, and not the shepherd, whose own the sheep are not, seeth the wolf coming, and leaveth the sheep, and fleeth: and the wolf catcheth them, and scattereth the sheep.

The hireling fleeth, because he is an hireling, and careth not for the sheep.

I am the good shepherd, and know my sheep, and am known of mine.

As the Father knoweth me, even so know I the Father: and I lay down my life for the sheep.

And other sheep I have, which are not of this fold: them also I must bring, and they shall hear my voice; and there shall be one fold, and one shepherd.

Therefore doth my Father love me, because I lay down my life, that I might take it again.

If we as pastors and ministers for the Lord are not teaching His people how to hear His voice, we are woefully neglecting our responsibilities. We should not be entrusted with a flock, for we have not the means to care for them. Only Jesus through the Holy Spirit can properly care for the flock, for they are His people and His alone. Without *rhema* revelation from Him, ministers are nothing and can do nothing. Hard facts, but it is better to hear them now, repent, and learn to live by every word of revelation that proceeds out of His mouth in order to properly care for the Lord's people. The judgment otherwise will be harsh and severe.

Remember: We each are members in particular in the body of Christ. We each have talents and abilities that He has given us or is willing to give us - spiritual talents and abilities that He can rise up in us to be able to serve in the body of Christ. Only the individual believer can fulfill that role, and the only way we will find out what that role is, is by learning to walk in "the way" of daily revelation from the Lord.

Israel flunked the Lord's curriculum in the wilderness. Jesus got an A+. May we learn to follow Him, and learn to be led by the Spirit that he gave to guide us in the way of the Lord.

Chapter 12

Ten Lessons from the Holy Spirit

One evening during the preparation of this book the Lord was building a great hunger in my heart to know the person of the Holy Spirit. During a telephone call, a brother in Christ prophesied that the Holy Spirit wanted to teach me a great many things, and that I was to spend much more time in my holy place, a secret place in the spirit, to learn from Him. It was clear that I needed to spend much more time there than I had been doing lately.

After the phone call, I immediately asked the Holy Spirit where He physically wanted me to go to find this holy place, and He said right on the floor of my bedroom where I was at the time would work just fine.

I got on my knees, my face to the floor. I began praising God, and after a short while the Holy Spirit began to speak into my spirit. He proceeded to reprove me with words that would be remarkably pointed and sharp to hear with my ears, but in the spirit realm they were a joy to receive. He told me to stop disobeying in my heart and to start trusting Him fully. Areas of mistrust came to mind such as how I had been resisting His power over me because of my past prejudices and teachings regarding the power and manifestations of the Holy Spirit, particularly during these end times.

The next morning in my office I again got on my knees to worship as I customarily do to start the day. As I settled down, the Spirit told me to first anoint the office with oil. Returning to my knees after doing so, He told me in my spirit that He is the servant to the King, and that He is here to do the will of the King (Jesus Christ). He told me that the King had sent Him because I had publicly confessed the fact that I have yielded my will to the King. Therefore the Holy Spirit was there to help me learn and receive all the things the King has prepared for me. Here are His words to me that morning. He proceeded to give me ten lessons.

Lesson I
"In order for Me to work (in you), it must be via joining your (own) will to Mine. I work in the spirit realm, and in order for you to work there too, your will must be joined to Mine. Then all the promises of the King can be brought to pass."

"Paul, we must spend much time together. The more you labor in the spirit with Me, the more you will accomplish for the King."

The Holy Spirit then told me to write these things down. They were much more beautifully told and received into my spirit than can be articulated on paper.

Lesson II
"I am Holy, and I am Spirit. I can be no other. I give life, and strength, and power to all who ask for it, who yield their will to the King. I am a servant. Those who desire to serve, will do so through me. Don't be flippant with Me, or take My working lightly. I am serious, and I am committed to carrying out the will of the King."

At this point I repented of having brushed aside the Holy Spirit at times, to which He responded that my repentance was the mark of a servant to the King. "The servant's heart is always and only to serve the King with determination and perseverance. Never quit carrying out the King's will."

Lesson III

"True servants are warriors. They are willing to endure hardship. They are always cognizant of their mission. Don't be surprised when you are called to do what seems impossible. Remember, I am your fellow servant because the King has sent Me to you. What (revelation from the Lord) seems impossible in the physical realm is not only possible, it is the will of Him who rules the universe. Therefore, don't ever doubt His will once you know what it is. My job is to help servants of the King carry them out. So be a warrior who refuses to give up."

Lesson IV

"No warrior can fight if he doesn't trust his master. Trust me completely because I work on trust. Remember, where your will separates from Me, I cannot work. So don't shut Me out by failing to trust Me. Nothing will happen to you that I do not know and allow beforehand."

Lesson V

Between each lesson, I realized I needed a fresh energizing from The Spirit, and to get it I was led to return to my knees and rest a while before sitting up to write.

"There is no will of self in heaven. All eyes, all hearts, all wills are directed toward the King. This is great joy. All worship and serve the King with joy. There is no room for self will."

Lesson VI

"My meat is to do the will of Him who sent Me. In eating this meat, you will find your sustenance. By eating from Him, i.e. discerning and then doing the King's will, you will be feeding from His table. This will cause you to grow great in your spirit."

At this point, my wife Rita entered the office with some homemade blueberry muffins and tea for breakfast. Still in the spirit, I said "God bless Rita", to which the Holy Spirit responded that she was also a servant of the King. "She has also been given to you so that you can better serve the King. The King selected her for you, and I am doing a mighty work in her that is separate from yours yet the two cannot be great without each other."

The Holy Spirit continued teaching about spiritual meat. "Some meat has to be chewed on for a while. Other meat is so tender it hardly needs chewing at all. But you must remember - the King provides the food. He selects it, and He directs its preparation."

Lesson VII

"You don't need to say anything when you are resting in the spirit realm. Let me minister to you. Warriors need a haven of rest, and they can only get it from Me in the spirit realm. Rest often in Me so I can minister to you. To carry the battle to victory, you must draw your strength from Me."

"You have learned to go to my holy place. But you must rest much more there so that I can teach you deep things of the Spirit. Rest in me. This is what Hebrews 3:7-4:16 is all about. There is a rest to God's people that few are using. I will lead them there if they will allow Me to."

Lesson VIII
"Look at your watch. How long have you been in school with Me today so far?" I looked at my watch and determined it had been fifty minutes.

"There is no time in the spirit realm. Consciousness of time when it comes to dining at the Master's table in the Holy Place does not exist. But when you are in the world, time becomes a stumbling block. So don't bring your watch into the spirit realm. You won't get the rest you need, you won't get the teaching you need, and you'll go out still carrying wounds from the battle. You can't afford that."

"Too many would-be warriors never learn that the rest in the Holy Spirit is for them. A yielded will can be taught things of the spirit, but an un-yielded will is too concerned with the world to be teachable for very long. Without staying for My ministering and teaching, they go too quickly back into battle. They become casualties. Sometimes they never recover. Don't carry a watch into My presence."

"I will tell you how to enter into My presence. I draw all men to the King. That's my job. But this is not only for salvation. It is my job to draw all men into fellowship at the table of the King. This job is much more demanding than simply getting the lost to become saved."

"Few there are who let me draw them into My rest because few there are who are willing to trust me enough to hear My voice in their spirit. Ask Me to show you how, and I will. I will show you how on everything that pertains to drawing closer to the King. This is My primary commission from Him."

Lesson IX

"So far I have called you a servant, and that is your calling. But you must remember that you are also a son of the Most High God. You are also a brother to His Son, the King, and the King has also called you His friend. Most of your activities will be in service to the King. This is the reason He sent Me to you – to help you serve. But don't forget, He longs to have friends like you. At His invitation, He has invited you to be His friend. This you have known for some time, but as you train for service, don't forget this friendship."

Lesson X

"Paul, I want you to include this visit with Me as the last chapter of your book. It's time to go, and you have service to do. You can return anytime, and there will be many times I will call you to your holy place so that I can teach and show you things of the spirit. But the door is always open to you at anytime. This is how I want to deal with servants of the King."

Remember:

1. To do anything for the Lord in the spirit realm, you must join your will to the will of the Holy Spirit.

2. Take the Holy Spirit very seriously. Never quit seeking and carrying out the will of the Lord, our King. The Holy Spirit will provide the strength and power to do the Lord's will if you ask for it.

3. Be a warrior who endures without giving up. Don't doubt the Lord's will for you once you discern it.

4. Trust the Holy Spirit completely.

5. There is no self will in heaven.

6. Eat (i.e. discern and do) what the Master gives you. Learn to eat from His table.

7. Enter His rest often. This is your refreshing for battle.

8. Don't carry your watch into the spirit realm. Dinner appointments should last as long as the Holy Spirit and the Lord direct.

9. Jesus is your Lord. Serve Him. He is also your friend. Be a friend to Him also.

10. Enter your secret place to be with the Holy Spirit. Let Him guide you to it. You have free access to Him 24 hours a day.

Appendix

Index of Scriptures

Endnotes

Endnotes

Chapter One: How I Learned to Hear the Voice of the Lord

[i] Paraphrased from <u>One Shall Chase a Thousand</u>, by Mabel Francis and Gerald B. Smith, 1997, Christian Publications, 3825 Hartzdale Drive, Camp Hill, PA 17011, pg. 137. The incident was originally reported in <u>The Alliance Witness</u>, February 27, 1974.

Chapter Two: How the Lord Can Build His Church Through You

[ii] Moulton, *Analytical Greek Lexicon*, Zondervan, 1978.

[iii] To study more about the field of binding and loosing, Liberty S. Savard's book, *Shattering Your Strongholds: Freedom From Your Struggles*, is highly recommended reading. Bridge-Logos Publishers, 1300 Airport Road Suite E, North Brunswick, NJ 08902, published in 1992.

[iv] I differentiate between Holy Spirit, the Giver, and His gift, holy spirit.

[v] A person can be born again and not speak in tongues. Lots of people have never been instructed, and are wonderful men and women for Christ. But for those who wish to walk more effectively in the power of the Spirit, tongues and all the other tools are needed. Every born again believer *can.* Many are simply held back by their own fears, lack of understanding, or the evil spirit of bondage noted in Romans 8:15.

[vi] Some believers refer to such anointings as long suits, others might call them special gifts or even spiritual phenomena.

Chapter Three: The Antidote to the Lukewarm Church

[vii] Bullinger, *Critical Lexicon and Concordance,* Zondervan 1976.
Strong's, *Exhaustive Concordance of the Bible,* MacDonald Publishing.
Moulton, *Analytical Greek Lexicon,* Zondervan 1978.

Endnotes

viii See Chapter Ten for a further discussion of this subject. Where a person yields his or her will, a door of entrance is open to satan. Other door openers include unconfessed sin, generational curses, self-imposed curses, etc. Possession is rarely total any more than yielding the will is total. "Demonized" is usually the preferred term rather than possession due to the fact that possession carries a sense of total control. More often than not with believers, demonic impact is partial. But regardless of which wording one agrees with, Christians will never arise to take their rightful position in the Lord's Army if they cannot deal with satan's sniper attacks.

Chapter Five: Would You Like Some More Manna, Son?

ix E.W. Bullinger, *Number in Scripture*, Kregel Publications, Grand Rapids, MI, 1978, p.235-242.

x The sin of Samaria specifically refers to the two golden calves set up by Jeroboam for worship in Dan and Bethel (I Kings 12:28; II Kings 10:29; 17:16; II Chronicles 11:15; 13:8). People succumbed to idol worship, and trusting sorcerers, enchanters, and other forms of the occult as a direct consequence of their failure to cultivate a revelation-manna providing relationship with the Lord.

Chapter Six: Eating the Bread of Life: How to Minister to the Lord

xi Copyright 1912 by The Rodeheaver Company, now in the public domain.

Chapter Seven: Become Confident in His Voice

xii According to II Corinthians 3:17-18, the Lord is that Spirit which not only brings understanding and takes away the veil over people's hearts, but He is also that Spirit which changes a person into His image. Communication may be received from the Father (Matthew 16:17), from Jesus Christ (John 10:27; Acts 9:10-16), and from the Holy Spirit (John 16:13; Acts 13:2). Note in

Endnotes

John 16:13 that the Holy Spirit speaks what He is told to speak. Only by revelation will a person know the difference. If it ever becomes an issue to you, why not ask Him? Regardless of which person of the Godhead speaks, there will be no cross purposes because all are of one mind.

[xiii] The authenticity of the concluding verses of Mark 16 has long been in question among scholars from schools of higher critical thought, but the evidence is overwhelming for their inclusion. For example, of the over 18 uncial and 600 cursive Greek manuscripts in existence, only two uncials and none of the cursives omit these verses.

Most all of the several versions in extent (many of which are considerably older than the extant Greek manuscripts) include these verses, most notably the oldest of them such as the Syriac Peshitta and Curetonian. The Latin versions, which are believed to have been sourced from manuscripts of earlier origin than the existing Greek manuscripts, contain these verses, as do the Gothic, Coptic (and all other Egyptian versions), the Armenian, Ethiopian, and Georgian versions.

Finally, over 100 early church fathers from 100 A.D. through 300 A.D. (including Justin Martyr, Irenaeus, Hyppolytus) and over two hundred such men from 300 A.D. through 600 A.D. (including Eusebius, Jerome, and Augustine) all referred to or quoted verses from this section of the Gospel of Mark. Cited from E.W.Bullinger, *The Companion Bible*, Zondervan, App 168; 1974.

Chapter Eight: Becoming Best Friends with the Lord

[xiv] Many records of the Old Testament can be viewed as "types" signifying our deliverance or behavior in a New Testament context. For example, the deliverance afforded through the red thread that Rehab hung out the window as a signal to Joshua's men in Jericho is often considered a type of the deliverance of Christ to the believers today. The apostle Paul used the "baptism" of God's people through the cloud and the Red Sea as a type of our baptism in Christ today (I Corinthians 10:1-4). The fourth man in the fiery furnace of Nebuchadnezzar is often used as a type of Christ's redemption, protection, and intercession.

Endnotes

---

xv Brown, Driver, Briggs, Gesenius, *The New Hebrew and English Lexicon,* Christian Copyrights, Inc., 1983

Strong's Exhaustive Concordance of the Bible, MacDonald Publishing Co.

Chapter Nine: Deception vs. Revelation: How to Discern the Difference

xvi A surprisingly tenacious and dangerous doctrine keeps popping up within Christian circles which denies that a person who is born-again of God's Holy Spirit can become possessed of an evil spirit. A more proper term, consistent with the excellent teaching of Derek Prince Ministries, is the word "demonized." See Chapter 10 for a more thorough treatment of this subject. Not only can a believer become demonized, i.e. influenced or controlled by demons, but it is so frequent a problem in the Christian church that the Holy Spirit gave discerning of spirits as a tool to detect them and Jesus Christ gave us the authority to bind them and cast them out. See also Kenneth Hagin's work, The Believer's Authority, Kenneth Hagin Ministries, PO Box 50126, Tulsa, OK 74150-0126, USA, and Rev. Dale M. Sides, "Exercising Spiritual Authority" books and seminar, Liberating Ministries For Christ International, PO Box 38, Bedford, VA 24523-0038, USA.

xvii I highly recommend Rev. Tim Sullivan's book, By the Grace of God I Am What I Am. Chapter 2, "A Fountain of Life", contains very helpful information for those desiring to grow in reverence, obedience and heart before the Lord. It is also extremely helpful in teaching how to avoid taking God for granted. A copy of this book may be obtained by contacting B.G. and E.T. Leonard Ministries, PO Box 3947, Brownsville, TX 78523-3947, USA. Used by permission.

Chapter Ten: How Can Believers Become Demonized?

xviii "To give heed" to seducing spirits in I Timothy 4:1 is the Greek word, *prosecho,* meaning to pay attention or regard to. It also may include the idea "to hold the mind", "be given to", "to give one's self up to", "to be addicted to", "to adhere to or be attached to". Clearly there is a will-yielding seduction process meant in this I Timothy 4:1, and it best characterizes one common way in which believers can become demonized in the church today.

Endnotes

Prosecho definition from Moulton's, *Analytical Greek Lexicon*, Zondervan, 1978.

[xix] It is tempting to equate the term "vexed" by an evil spirit with possession, influence, demonized, etc. The purpose of this chapter is to show Biblically that Christians <u>can</u> become demonically afflicted, not to get lost in finding an inoffensive, Biblically acceptable term to describe it. There is no Scriptural indication that such affliction has ceased affecting the church today. Healing from sickness is still a need within the church, and so is deliverance from demons. The reader may wish to pursue other excellent reference materials published on this subject such as those by Derek Prince Ministries, P.O. Box 19501, Charlotte, NC 28219-9501, USA.

[xx] The same argument is equally true in the field of breaking generational, witchcraft, and self-imposed curses over believers. For further understanding of this field, generally referred to as a deliverance ministry, I recommend the work of Pastor Carl Fox, of Christian Faith International, Shekanah Lane, Huntingdon, TN 38344, USA.

Chapter Eleven: The Way of the Lord

[xxi] See Numbers 12:1-8 in which the Lord lists five ways that He speaks to men. For further discussion of this subject, see John and Paula Sandford's excellent book, <u>The Elijah Task</u>, Victory House, PO Box 700238, Tulsa, OK 74170.

[xxii] For further discussion and depth in the area of teaching children to walk by the Spirit, the reader is encouraged to study the materials offered by Pastors David and Kathie Walters of Goodnews Fellowship Ministries, Route 28 Box 95D, Macon, GA 31210.

About the Author

One of the greatest pieces of advice I have ever read concerning ministry work came from Oral Roberts' autobiography. He gave a ten-point admonition to ministers, and I have never failed to grow especially thankful for the first one whenever I hear it: "I discovered that the message is greater than the messenger." I would like to pass this same thought along to all the readers of this book because, as the Lord continues to work with each of us providing revelation manna, it is so easy to fall prey to pride.

I have numerous and significant credentials in secular and non-secular academics, pastoral as well as worldly professional accomplishments. I am grateful for the background that I have. It is not false humility to abstain from the temptation of listing them. It is simply that they make no difference, and I'd much rather the reader remember the message than the messenger.

One night, as I was getting ready to go to sleep, the Lord asked me, "Paul, do you want a worldwide ministry, or do you want to see the Word of God go over the world?" It was clear in my spirit that the Lord was happy to do either one. He gave me to understand that by worldwide ministry, he meant a high profile, stadium-filling ministry. I thought a moment to check myself, but my immediate heart-reaction was, and still remains today, to move the Word of God over the world and to do it His way, not mine. "Good," He replied. "I knew you would say that. And because you did, I will bring people to you to teach, people for whom I will fill those stadiums, and people who will cause My Word to move over the world."

I cried a long time that night. This book is meant to be about growing in relationship with Jesus Christ. All I am and all I hope to be is to be found in Him, that the glory may be His, and His alone. May you be one of those Whom He enables to move His Word to the nations, whether through large and high visibility ministry, or through walking with one or two of His precious children on their roads to Emmaus, helping their hearts to be One with the Shepherd.

To Order More Copies of this Book....

Additional copies of *Dining at the Master's Table: Learning to Hear the Voice of the Lord* or other books and publications may be ordered using the order form at the back of this book:

Kingdom Faith Ministries
PO Box 725
Charlemont, MA 01339
USA
Tel: (413) 339-8630
Email: Kingdom8@Juno.com
Web: http://www.kingdomfaith.org

Other books by Paul Norcross:

- ### Succeeding in Spiritual Warfare
  A detailed view of spiritual warfare principles from Joshua. This is a book most believers warn not to begin reading at night – most stay up all night to absorb what the Holy Spirit energizes in the hearts of the people who read this book. $15 plus shipping.

- ### The Voice Upon The Waters
  A continuation of things the Lord taught Pastor Norcross since writing Dining At The Master's Table. $5 plus shipping

- ### Marriage Seminar: How To Walk By The Spirit In Your Marriage
  A seminar and detailed study book which applies the truths of learning to hear the voice of the Lord in marriages to make them as vibrant a reflection of the mystery of godliness as God intended. The strength of every church rests in the strength of the marriages within the church. $50 plus shipping.

- ### Acts 29 Course: How To Walk By The Spirit (Vol I, II, and III)
  A series of student workbooks which train students to understand and operate all nine manifestation gifts of the Holy Spirit. Extensive focus on developing deep intimacy with Jesus Christ, followed by careful Scriptural development of proficiency in each supernatural gift of the Holy Spirit. $15 each vol plus ship.

- ### Breaking The Authority Of The Bastard Curse: Restoring The Congregation of the Lord (Co-Authored with Carl L. Fox; $10 plus ship)
  The only curse in the Bible which lasts for 10 generations, it is mentioned in both Deuteronomy and Hebrews. Hidden, but powerful enough to cause continuing rebellion and patterns of offenses within the church, this book teaches how to receive deliverance from its long-reaching generational effects.

Learning To Hear The Voice Of The Lord

A six cassette tape series covering how to hear the voice of the Lord. This conference offers dynamic preaching of this inspiring topic to help God's people grow confident in their relationship and intimacy with Him.   *$30 plus $5.00 shipping and handling.*

Finding and Flowing in Your Anointing

Offers a unique and vibrant challenge to find and flow in the anointing God will give you to carry out His plan for you. These tapes speak to how you can determine and pursue God's destiny for you. Your anointing is going to cost you everything. Find out how to receive it in this powerful and prophetic three-tape series. *$20 plus $5.00 shipping and handling.*

Marriage Seminar: How To Be Led By The Spirit In Your Marriage

A six tape series which enables couples to break free of spiritual bondage and old wounds, gain their healing and learn to make their marriage a glory to God – by the Spirit and not by the flesh. Includes balancing ministry and family, breaking ungodly soul ties, cleansing the home of cursed objects, and hearing the voice of the Lord to provide direction and blessings to the whole family. Includes full study syllabus.   *$50 plus $7.00 shipping and handling.*

*For information on how to schedule a live seminar in your area,
please contact Kingdom Faith Ministries*

Kingdom Faith Ministries
Resource Materials Order Form

To order materials, please send a copy of this order form with your check or money order, or call us at (413) 339-8630, or e-mail us at kingdom8@juno.com .

ITEM	QUANTITY	PRICE/EACH	TOTAL
Dining At The Master's Table: Learning to Hear The Voice Of The Lord	_____	$12.00	_____
Audio Tape Set	_____	$15.00	_____
How To Succeed In Spiritual Warfare: Lessons From Joshua	_____	$15.00	_____
The Voice Upon The Waters	_____	$ 5.00	_____
Breaking The Authority of The Bastard Curse: Restoring The Congregation of the Lord	_____	$10.00	_____
Acts 29 Course: How To Walk By The Spirit (Volume I Workbook)	_____	$15.00	_____
Volume II Workbook	_____	$15.00	_____
Volume III Workbook	_____	$15.00	_____
Marriage Seminar: How To Walk By The Spirit In Your Marriage (Audio Tape Set and Student Syllabus)	_____	$50.00	_____
	SUBTOTAL		_____
	SHIPPING & HANDLING		_____
	TOTAL		_____

Name

Shipping Address

City   State   Zip Code   Country

SHIPPING/HANDLING RATES FOR ORDERS In USA (shipped priority mail where possible)
1-2 Books/Tape Sets $5.00   3-4 Books/Tape Sets $10.00
5-6 Books/Tape Sets $15.00   7-8 Books/Tape Sets $20.00
MAIL CHECK OR MONEY ORDERS TO:
Kingdom Faith Ministries
PO Box 725
Charlemont, MA 01339
214